# Praise for Weird and Wacky Holiday Marketing Guide Through the Years ...

"This book is a fun way to market just about anything. Organized by month, with month-long holidays, week-long holidays, and then daily holidays. Most of the holidays are so obscure that a vast majority of people wouldn't be aware they even exist. But that is the point: taking a weird & wacky holiday and making a fun marketing post with it.

"Behind the monthly holidays is a section with sample posters and additional ideas that can be transferred to any other holiday, a sample press release, as well as links to companies and social media sites that might also help.

"I have gone through and highlighted holidays I want to promote for fun next time they roll around. The title is all about having a little fun while you market, and this book will not disappoint."

**—Pat Stanford, Author and Poet (2019 Edition)**

Ginger Marks' books are AMAZING! Her Marketing Guide is a MUST HAVE for those wanting their products to stand out in a crowd. All her books are wonderful. Ginger's Marketing Book is a PERFECT solution to all my sales and marketing needs. Don't miss out on her unique Marketing TIPS to think outside the box and stand out in a crowd. Thank you, Ginger!

**—Jennifer P., Author/Illustrator (2019 Edition)**

"Ginger Marks' *Weird and Wacky Holiday Marketing Guide* is a compendium of ideas to market your product, tying it to state, national, and international celebrations of every conceivable kind. The research done for this book is mind-boggling. The holidays are organized by month, and list month-long, week-long, and daily holidays. Appendix A provides a huge number of ready-made materials you can use for blog posts, flyers, press releases, etc. If you're looking to jump-start your marketing, you must get this book. Highly recommended."

**—A Writer (2018 Edition)**

"A Google search on Steroids! Have you ever done a Google search while preparing a presentation and found an incredible list that helped you add lots of ideas to what you were doing? I have and know that having such a list always gives me lots of information to make my presentation more interesting and colorful.

"Ginger Marks' *2018 Weird and Wacky Holiday Marketing Guide* is just like having the results of a Google search, only it is like having such a list on steroids! The guide contains an overwhelming number of marketing ideas. The first 70 pages list national, international, and often quirky and humorous events which take place throughout the year, listed in month-to-month order. If humor is what you are looking for, you will learn that National Hermit Week falls in June, "Hot Enough for Ya Day" falls on July 23$^{rd}$, and August 7$^{th}$ is known as the "Particularly Preposterous Packaging Day." These three dates are samples of the hundreds (even maybe a thousand) of weird & wacky celebrations, festivals, and events that are included in Ginger Marks' 2018 guide.

"The second half of the book contains several appendices, which provide all kinds of marketing information. I can't imagine a business owner who couldn't find some great marketing ideas while looking through the first half of this book, or who couldn't find links to companies that might help his or her business in the second half of the book. There is so much information here. The *2018 Weird and Wacky Holiday Marketing Guide* is a terrific resource!"

**—Gary Ciesla (2018 Edition)**

"As someone who's taught 'Marketing Your Biz on a Shoestring' for years, I always note the value of fun/crazy/unusual holidays for adding to your marketing options. Ginger has put together a great guide that gives you EVERYTHING: serious holidays, regularly scheduled holidays, and just for fun stuff."

**—Wendy Meyeroff, WM Medical Communications, Inc. (2018 Edition)**

"Ginger Marks has put together a fantastic resource! If you are looking for outside of the box ideas for marketing as well as for celebrating, you will love the *Weird and Wacky Holiday Marketing Guide.* As a former elementary school teacher, I wish I had had a copy of this incredible resource when I was teaching. The month-long and week-long holidays, listed throughout this guide, could create the foundation for exciting study units."

**—D'vorah Lansky, M.Ed. Best-Selling author of** *Book Marketing Made Easy*, **www. BookMarketingMadeEasy.com (2016 Edition)**

"Great marketing tools for social media business exposure. Having multiple businesses and managing websites, I found this book to be a wonderful asset for trying to come up with new *and different* ideas for marketing, especially on social media. Talk about having every holiday imaginable listed in this book! There are also so many that it intrigues your interest to go off and investigate on your own, after learning about them for the first time.

"I personally liked that at the end of the calendar month Ginger adds some ideas on how to use these holidays to your advantage in marketing, but more importantly, she is always adding comments like, you can raise the money for charity or a good cause (not just to market your business but also help your community at the same time). If you have a business that is seeking attention on social media, I know this book will help you announce some totally 'Weird & Wacky' facts for every day of the year, that will certainly get you noticed! There's a wealth of resources here."

**—Cheryl (2018 Edition)**

"So much info in one book! As a business owner, it's difficult to stand out. With Ginger's guidance you can set yourself apart from the crowd. It's well-written and easy to follow. Tons and tons of info and well worth it!"

**—Patti Knoles, Virtual Graphic Arts Department (2017 Edition)**

"Awesome very practical and fun marketing ideas. Ginger Marks' *2018 Weird and Wacky Holiday Marketing Guide* is an amazing book and tool for me to use preparing speeches in my business. Using anecdotes from the book I can enhance my presentations to be much more fun and colorful and keep the audience entertained. I can't wait to show this book to my colleagues.

"There are numerous marketing ideas I never would have come up with on my own that I plan to use in my business, social media, which should really help engagement. I love that I can get new ideas all year long!"

**—Rachel I (2018 Edition)**

# 2022 *Weird & Wacky* 13th Edition
# HOLIDAY MARKETING GUIDE

### Your business marketing calendar of ideas

## Ginger Marks

**DocUmeant** *Publishing*

244 5th Avenue
Suite G-200
NY, NY 10001
646-233-4366

*www.DocUmeantPublishing.com*

2022 Weird and Wacky Holiday Marketing Guide, Volume 14

**Published by**
DocUmeant Publishing
244 5th Ave, Ste G–200

NY, NY 10001

646-233-4366

Editor Philip S. Marks

Layout and Design Ginger Marks
DocUmeant Designs
www.DocUmeantDesigns.com

Library of Congress: 2022930264

ISBN: 978-1-950075-72-0

ePub: 978-1-950075-73-7

ASIN: B09P9KQQD1

# Contents

# Introduction

Events are one of the smartest antidotes for slumping sales and for maintaining a healthy business. It's not enough anymore to merely have goods on the shelf and open the doors on time every day. We all need to reinvent our businesses to keep them thriving and healthy. And that is just what this book helps you achieve.

This unique marketing book continues to win awards year after year and remains a #1 Best-Seller in the Business Marketing genre. Highly praised by marketing experts and in its second decade, this annual book offers more fun and easy marketing ideas exclusively penned for the calendar year 2022. Now you can grow your business with strategies built around wacky holidays, observed throughout the world, for the entire 2022 calendar year. If you missed the premier 2009 issue or want to complete your collection, all previous and unique yearly editions are available at http://www.HolidayMarketingGuide.com.

As *Weird & Wacky Holiday Marketing Guide* is read and used internationally, I have included many international holidays. Also, it was brought to my attention that it was a bit difficult to decipher the individual holidays in the daily listings. So, rather than using a comma to separate each one, I have used a bullet. What do you think? Should I keep the bullet? Is it easier to identify the daily holidays? Email me at ginger.marks@DocUmeantDesigns.com and let me know.

To take advantage of the information provided, pick a day and discover the unusual holidays celebrated on that date. Then, read the corresponding month's "Holiday Marketing Ideas" section to find a simple implementation or allow it to open your creative mind and think of some of your own.

Please note that the asterisk (*) in front of a holiday means a specific holiday is celebrated on that numerical date each year. For example, Christmas Day is December 25 no matter what day that falls on during the calendar week.

Here's another exceptional marketing idea for you I discovered when visiting BrownieLocks. com back in 2009, and which is now listed in the official *Chase Calendar of Events* which I cull from every year. Bonza Bottler Days™—the day is the same as the month it is in. That equates to: 1/1, 2/2, 3/3, etc. There is one in every month. There you have it; another extra fine excuse for an event to boost your notoriety and sales each and every month!

This is by no means a comprehensive edition. I have made all attempts to ensure the accuracy of the contents. If you encounter errors or know of a holiday that needs to be included, please let me know so they can be addressed in future editions. But remember, if your suggested holiday addition is not listed in the official *Chase Calendar of Events* it is not eligible for inclusion. If you want it to be, contact *Chase Calendar of Events* learn how to get your favorite holiday included.

Read on, have fun, initiate your own version of these holidays, and reap the benefit for your business.

Ginger Marks

Companion
Playbook for

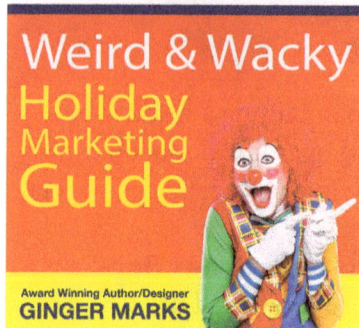

Weird & Wacky
Holiday
Marketing
Guide

Award Winning Author/Designer
GINGER MARKS

P.S. The *Weird and Wacky Holiday Marketing Companion Playbook*. This tool is intended to help you to create, organize, and put the FUN back into your marketing plan. Each monthly calendar offers space for you to begin your planning and keep all your notes in one handy book. Since each year the physical calendar days rotate, I have left the date numbers blank to enable you to make use of this *Companion Playbook* beginning today.

# Annual Dates of Note

## United Nations International Year of Glass

In a resolution made May 18, 2022, the General Assembly declared this year for 2022, recognizing "that, as one of the most important, versatile and transformative materials of history, glass is an important component in many areas." For info: United Nations. Web: www.un.org.

## International Year of Artisanal Fisheries and Aquaculture

In a resolution made Dec 5, 2017, the General Assembly declared this year for 2022 with the Food and Agriculture Organization serving as the lead agency. This year calls attention to both sustainable economies as they relate to fishing and the need to conserve aquatic life and ecosystems and reduce related pollution. For info: United Nations. Web: www.un.org.

## Chinese Year of the Tiger[1]

2022 is the Year of the Tiger according to Chinese zodiac. This is a Year of Water Tiger, starting from the 2022 Chinese New Year on Feb. 1 and lasting to 2023 Lunar New Year's Eve on Jan. 21. The Tiger ranks third in the 12-year cycle of the Chinese zodiac signs. The Years of the Tiger include 1914, 1926, 1938, 1950, 1962, 1974, 1986, 1998, 2010, 2022, 2034 . . .

Tigers, considered to be brave, cruel, forceful, and terrifying, are the symbol of power and lordliness in Chinese culture. In ancient times, people usually compared

1    Travel China Guide. https://www.travelchinaguide.com/intro/social_customs/zodiac/tiger.htm

emperors or kings with the tigers. Tigers are also considered as a patron deity for children and parents will prepare the shoes and hats with tiger designs for their babies.

The Chinese zodiac Tiger sign entitles people born in the Years of the Tiger to be natural leaders. They are adventurous, ambitious, and have a strong sense of justice, but maybe also a little arrogant and impetuous.

## Lucky Signs

Lucky Numbers: 1, 3, 4

Lucky Colors: gray, blue, white, orange

Lucky Flowers: cineraria, anthurium

## Lucky Directions

South, east, southeast

## Strengths

Brave, passionate, optimistic, love challenges and adventures

## Weaknesses

Rebellious, overconfident, stubborn, emotional

## Best Jobs and Careers

Best Jobs: Politician, economist, adventurer, banker, doctor, police officer, lawyer ...

As the Tigers are born leaders, they have an excellent organization ability and brilliant communication skills, and thus becoming a successful politician will be less difficult compared to others. Besides the ability to lead, they are also confident, fearless, and face various challenges with lower anxiety, so that adventurers and bankers are among the best jobs for the Tigers. They also like mathematics, think logically, and have flexible minds, all of which help them to win a job like an economist

Best Working Partners: Horse, Dog, Pig

Best Age to Start a Business: 35 – 50

Best Career Fields: Politics

## Matches

Dragon, Horse, Pig

Tigers are so talkative, so if people want to make friends with them, they need to learn to be patient listeners first. They are also quite confident and always feel good about themselves, so people should not point out their mistakes or flaws in public. Otherwise, they will form grudges and take revenge. They like to win and never lose, even in a very small competition. People should avoid stealing their thunder in unnecessary occasions. They are also accustomed to a dominant role in decision making. When proposing advice, it is better to use a convincing and tactful way to express your thoughts.

## Avoid: Ox, Tiger, Snake, Monkey

Ox: One depends on the other financially, but their values towards money are different. Therefore, they may quarrel on the money problem.

Tiger: Both of them are mighty, wanting to be in a dominant role and take control of the other in marriage. They never want to make compromises.

Snake: They like scheming and guessing each other's minds, and it's hard for them to open their hearts. They lack faith in each other and have little in common.

Monkey: They may get together for power or profit, but not out of love. Relationship without love cannot go far. And they may stand against each other because of interest dispute.

## Tiger's Personality by Blood Type

*Blood Type O:* Tigers with blood type O are warm-hearted and develop a good sense of justice. They are never afraid of failures and can always hold their own.

*Blood Type A:* For those with blood type A, they may have completely contrary characteristics at the same time, sometimes active and progressive, but sometimes shy and conservative.

*Blood Type B:* They love making friends and are specializing in social interactions. However, the overemotional personality sometimes makes them lack planning.

*Blood Type AB:* They are positive and confident, good at convincing others, which helps to get great success at work. But it may be a bit hard for them to follow through.

# JANUARY

Jan 6 – Mar 1 Carnival Season
Jan 20 – Feb 19 Aquarius the Water Carrier

## Month-Long Holidays

Be Kind to Food Servers Month • Book Blitz Month • Get Organized and Be Productive Month • International Child-Centered Divorce Month • International Creativity Month • National Clean Up Your Computer Month • National Conscience Month • National Glaucoma Awareness Month • National Hot Tea Month • National Mentoring Month • National Radon Action Month • National Slavery and Human Trafficking Prevention Month • National Volunteer Blood Donor Month • Oatmeal Month • Worldwide Rising Star Month

## Week-Long Holidays

Jan 1 – 2 Taiwan: Foundation Days

Jan 3 – 9 Dating and Life Coach Recognition Week

Jan 9 – 15 Idiom Week

Jan 11 – 17 Cuckoo Dancing Week

Jan 15 – 16 Bald Eagle Appreciation Days

Jan 16 – 22 Hunt for Happiness Week

Jan 18 – 25 Week of Christian Unity

Jan 23 – 29 Clean Out Your Inbox Week • Snowcare for Troops Awareness Week

## Daily Holidays

1. *Bonza Bottler Day™ • Canada: Polar Bear Swim 2022 • *Copyright Revision Law Signed (1976) • Cuba: Liberation Day • Czech-Slovak Divorce (1993) • *Ellis Island Opened (1892) • *Emancipation Proclamation Takes Effect (1863) • *Euro Introduced (1999) • *First Baby Boomer Born (1946) • *Frankenstein (1818) • *Haiti: Independence Day • *National Environmental Policy Act (1970) • *New Year's Day • *Paul Revere Birthday (1735) • *Betsy Ross (1752) • Russia New Year's Day Observance • Saint Basil's Day • Sudan: Independence Day • *Z Day

2. 55-MPH Speed Limit (1974) • Isaac Asimov Birth (1920) • Distinguished Service Medal Day • Haiti: Ancestor's Day • *Happy Mew Year for Cats Day • Japan: Kakizome • Switzerland: Berchtoldstag

3. Memento Mori, Saint Geneviève Feast Day • National Thank God It's Monday Day • JRR Tolkien Birth (1892)

4. *Amnesty for Polygamists (1893) • *Louise Braille Birth (1809) • *Dimpled Chad Day • Earth at Perihelion, *Myanmar: Independence Day • *Isaac Newton Birth (1643) • *Pop Music Chart Introduced (1936) • *Trivia Day • *World Braille Day • World's Tallest Building Dedicated (2010)

5. *Alvin Ailey Birth (1931) • *Five-Dollar-a-Day Minimum Wage Day (1914) • National Bird Day • Twelfth Night

6. *Armenian Christmas • *Epiphany or Twelfth Day • *Three Kings Day

7. *First Balloon Fight Across the English Channel (1785) • *International Programmers' Day • Japan: Nanakusa • *National Bobblehead Day • Orthodox Christmas • Russia: Christmas Observed • Transatlantic Phoning (1927)

8. Argyle Day • Greece: Midwife's Day or Women's Day • *National Joygerm Day • *Show-and-Tell at Work Day • *War on Poverty (1964)

9. *Aviation in America (1793) • *Panama: Martyrs' Day • Switzerland: Meitlisunntic

10. England: Plough Monday, Japan: Coming-of-Age Day • League of Nations Founding (1920) • National Clean-Off-Your-Desk Day • Women's Suffrage Amendment Introduced in Congress (1878)

11. Morocco: Independence Day • Nepal: National Unity Day • Poetry at Work Day • U.S. Surgeon General Declares Cigarettes Hazardous (1964)

12. Batman Day • *Haiti Earthquake Day (2010) • National Hot Tea Day • Tanzania: Zanzibar Revolution Day

13. Norway: Tyvendedagen • *Radio Broadcasting Day (1910) • Russian Old New Year's Eve • Sweden: St. Knut's Day • Togo: Liberation Day

14. *Arnold Benedict Day • *Ratification Day • Uzbekistan: Army Day • World Logic Day

15. *Alpha Kappa Alpha Sorority Day • National Bagel Day • National Use Your Gift Card Day

16. *Appreciate a Dragon Day • *Civil Service Day • El Salvador: National Day of Peace • Japan Haru-No-Yabuiri, Malawi: John Chilembwe Day • National Nothing Day • National Quinoa Day • *Religious Freedom Day

17. Anne Brontë Day • The Business of America Quote Day (1925) • *Cable Car Day (1871) • *Al Capone Day • *Ben Franklin Day (1706) • International Mentoring Day • Japan: Earthquake Day • *Judgment Day • Kid Inventors' Day • Martin Luther King, Jr. Birth Observed (1986) • Mexico: Blessing of the Animals at the Cathedral • Poland: Liberation Day • Popeye Day • Quarterly Estimated Federal Income Tax Day (also Apr 15, Jun 15, and Sep 15) • Saint Anthony's Day • Southern California Earthquake Day (1994) • Tu B'Shvat

18. Lewis and Clark Day • *Pooh Day

19. Ethiopia: Timket • Robert E. Lee Day • National Popcorn Day • Edgar Allen Poe Day

20. Azerbaijan: Martyrs' Day • Brazil: San Sebastian's Day • Get to Know Your Customers Day (third Thursday of each quarter is set aside to get to know your customers even better) • Guinea-Bissau:

National Heroes Day • Lesotho: Army Day • US Hostages in Iran Released (1981) • US Revolutionary War Ends Day (1783)

21. Arbor Day in Florida • First Supersonic Concorde Flight (1976) • Hat Day • International Fetish Day • Kiwanis International Founding (1915) • National Hug Your Puppy Day • *National Hugging Day

22. *Answer Your Cat's Question Day • Laugh-In Day • *Roe vs. Wade Decision (1973) • *Saint Vincent: Feast Day • Ukraine: Ukrainian Day

23. Bulgaria: Babin Den (Midwives/Grandmother's Day) • *National Handwriting Day • National Pie Day • Snowplow Mailbox Hockey Day

24. *Belly Laugh Day • California Gold Discovery Day • *Beer Can Day (1935) • *National Compliment Day • United Nations: International Day of Education • World Day for African and Afrodescendant Culture

25. *Around the World in 72 Days (1890) • *Macintosh Debuts (1984) • *A Room of One's Own Day • Saint Dwynwen's Day

26. Australia: Australia Day • Dental Drill Day • Dominican Republic: National Holiday, India: Republic Day • Gujarat India Earthquake (2001) • Rocky Mountain National Park Day

27. Canadian Caper/Operation Argo (1980) • Leningrad Liberated (1944) • *Mozart Day • National Geographic Society Founded (1888) • *Thomas Crapper Day • United Kingdom: *Vietnam Peace Day

28. *Challenger Space Shuttle Explosion (1986) • Data Privacy Day • Israeli Siege of Suez City Ends (1974) • National Preschool Fitness Day

29. *Curmudgeons' Day • W.C. Fields Day • National Seed Swap Day • *Seeing Eye Dog Day

30. Ireland: Bloody Sunday (50th Anniversary, 1972) • Inane Answering Message Day • National Croissant Day • World Leprosy Day

31. Bubble Wrap® Appreciation Day • *First Social Security Check Issued (1940) • The Grammy Awards • *Inspire Your Heart with the Arts Day • Nauru: National Holiday

# Holiday Marketing Ideas

**National Clean Up Your Computer Month** — These days it is nigh impossible to have a computer with no viruses or malware. However, our computers also tend to run out of free disc space. So, cleaning up your computer of unnecessary files and unused programs will go a long way to assisting you to clean up your computer.

If you happen to be a computer guru, you could promote your business by offering a web-based seminar teaching others what to look out for and how to fix the most common computer ailments. If you aren't a pro, sponsor or host the seminar!

Social media tips and infographics can also boost your business' fingerprint when you add your branding and logo to them. You have an entire month to share your wisdom, so post often and engage your visitors.

You'll find an infographic provided by Wondershare in the Samples Appendix that you can share. If you want to brand one to your business and need my assistance, contact me at ginger.marks@DocUmeantDesigns.com and I'll be happy to assist you.

**Jan 4 World Braille Day** — Do you realize that, in the US approximately 2.4% of the population is visually impaired? That doesn't seem like a lot until you realize that partial to total blindness affects 7,894,900 Americans.

According to nfb.org each year, the American Printing House for the Blind (APH) polls each state for data on the number of legally blind children (through age twenty-one) enrolled in elementary and high school in the US eligible to receive free reading matter in Braille, large print, or audio format. That equates to Braille readers: 4,963 (7.8%) Print readers: 20,460 (32.3%).[2]

Those are the facts. Now, how can you utilize this day to market your business? Blindness can also indicate your customers' and clients' inability to understand everything you have to offer, or even something they want to learn how to do or do better. Therefore, consider putting together a group of pros who can share on topics that they want to hear about. This can be done in person or online, whichever you are comfortable in this present day COVID-19 environment.

Of course, other things you can do always include social media offerings. Things like stats, blindness prevention, and the like are all good starting points.

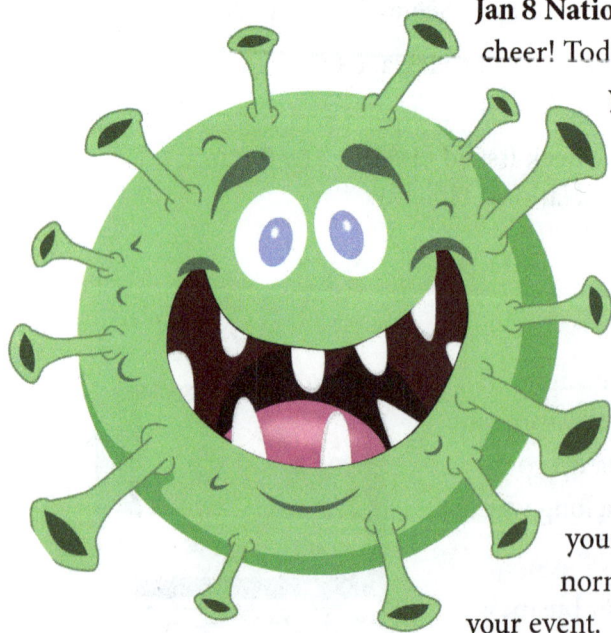

**Jan 8 National JoyGerm Day** — This fun holiday is all about spreading cheer! Today love abounds. Infect as many people as you can with your happiness and cheer. Share a smile with those around you and have some fun in the process as you promote your business. How so? Simple, hand out a card wishing everyone you meet a Happy National JoyGerm Day that is branded to your business. Better yet, hand out bite-sized candy bars wrapped with your banded label, or even a chocolate kiss with your message attached. You'll find samples in the Appendix.

Another fine way to celebrate is to host an online party! As the host or even the sponsor of events you'll be getting your name in front of a whole host of peeps that you wouldn't normally have access to as your speakers will help you promote your event.

---

2    American Printing House for the Blind, "Annual Report 2017: Distribution of Eligible Students Based on the Federal Quota Census of January 4, 2016 (Fiscal Year 2016)." Retrieved from http://www.aph.org/federal-quota/distribution-of-students-2017 .

**Jan 12 National Hot Tea Day**— This one I envision as either handing out branded tea bags or having a tea party. Local events would be perfect for this. However, you most certainly could have an online tea party! I have a client whose whole business is based on tea who has successfully hosted those types of events.

Thinking about what tea represents, I am reminded that wrapping your hands around an aromatic, beautifully decorated tea cup engenders calmness. So, stress relief could also be a viable topic. If not an event, then at least share facts about stress or tips on how to reduce or eliminate it from your life? And then there's always the medical side of things to consider.

**Jan 24 National Compliment Day** — How does it make you feel when you get complimented? Consider the impact you could have when you take a moment to look for the good in others and let them know how unique and special they are.

One sure way to market your business as you celebrate today is to snail mail a card to your most loyal customers to let them know you appreciate them. If you know them well enough — which if they are loyal to you, you certainly should — give them a heartfelt compliment about something you appreciate about them. An email will suffice to get this done, but a note or card will have so much more of an impact than a quickly read and disregarded email will have.

# FEBRUARY

Feb 28 – Mar 1 Germany: Munich Fasching Carnival
Feb 10 – 20 Germany: Berlin International Film Festival

## Month-Long Holidays

African American Cultural Heritage Month • AMD/Low Vision Awareness Month • American Heart Month • Bake for Family Fun Month • Feline Fix by Five Month • Library Lovers' Month • Marfan Syndrome Awareness Month • National African American History Month • National Bird-Feeding Month • National Black History Month • National Cherry Month • National Children's Dental Health Month • National Goat Yoga Month • National Mend a Broken Heart Month • National Pet Dental Health Month • National Time Management Month • Plant the Seeds of Greatness Month • Return Shopping Carts to the Supermarket Month • Spay/Neuter Awareness Month • Wise Health Care Consumer Month • Worldwide Renaissance of the Heart Month

## Week-Long Holidays

Feb 1 – 7 United Nations: World Interfaith Harmony Week
Feb 6 – 12 Dump Your "Significant Jerk" Week
Feb 6 – 13 Freelance Writers Appreciation Week
Feb 8 – 10 World AG Expo
Feb 13 – 19 Love a Mensch Week
Feb 14 – 20 International Flirting Week
Feb 18 – 21 Great Backyard Bird Count
Feb 20 – 26 Build a Better Trade Show Image Week • National Engineers Week

## Daily Holidays

1. Car Insurance Day • Chinese New Year • *Robinson Crusoe Day • Freedom Day • G.I. Joe Day • Greensboro Sit-In (1960) • Space Shuttle *Columbia* Disaster (2003) • St. Laurent/Louis Stephen Day

2. *Bonza Bottler Day™ • *Candlemas Day or Presentation of the Lord, *Groundhog Day • Hedgehog Day • *Imbolc, Luxembourg: Candlemas, Mexico: Dia de la Candelaria • National Girls and Women in Sports Day • National Signing Day • *The Record of a Sneeze" (1893) • Sled Dogs Save Nome (1925)

3. *"The Day the Music Died" (1959) • *Four Chaplains Memorial Day • Mozambique: Heroes' Day • Veterinary Pharmacist Day • Vietnam: National Holiday

4. Angola: Armed Struggle Day • Apache Wars Begin (1868) • Bubble Gum Day • *Facebook Launches (2004) • Medjool Date Day • National Wear Red Day • *Rosa Parks Birthday (1913) • Sri Lanka: Independence Day • United Nations: International Day of Human Fraternity • *USO Founded (1941) • World Cancer Day

5. *Family Leave Bill Signing (1993) • Longest War in History Ends • Mexico: Constitution Day • Take Your Child to the Library Day • *Weatherperson's Day

6. New Zealand: Waitangi Day • "Babe" Ruth Birthday (1895) • Switzerland: Homstom • United Nations: International Day of Zero Tolerance for Female Genital Mutilation

7. *Chaplin's "Tramp" Day (1914) • *Charles Dickens (1812) • Grenada: Independence Day • Abraham Lincoln Day • National Black HIV/AIDS Awareness Day • *Wave Your Fingers at Your Neighbor Day

8. *Boy Scouts of America Day (1910) • Extraterrestrial Culture Day • Japan: Hari-Kuyo (Festival of Broken Needles) • Slovenia: Culture Day

9. *Beatles Day (1964) • *Gypsy Rose Lee (1914) • Lebanon: Saint Maron's Day • National Pizza Day • Read in the Bathtub Day

10. *"All the News That's Fit to Print" Slogan (1897) • *First Computer Chess Victory over Human (1996) • *Charles Lamb (1775) • *Plimsoll Day • Treaty of Paris (1763) • United Nations: World Pulses Day • *WWII Medal of Honor (1942)

11. Cameroon: Youth Day • *Thomas Edison Birthday (1847) • *First Woman Episcopal Bishop (1989) • Get Out Your Guitar Day • Iran: Victory of Islamic Revolution • *Japan: National Foundation Day • Nelson Mandela Prison Release Day (1990) • *National Shut-In Visitation Day • *Pro Sports Wives Day • *Satisfied Staying Single Day • United Nations: International Day of Women and Girls in Science • Vatican City: Independence Day • White Shirt Day

12. *Dracula Day • *International Darwin Day • Abraham Lincoln Birthplace Cabin Wreath Laying Day • Myanmar: Union Day • NAACP Founded (1909) • *Oglethorpe Day • *Safetypup® Birthday • Utah: Women Given the Vote (1870)

13. Dresden Firebombing (1945) • Employee Legal Awareness Day • *First Magazine Published in America (1741) • Galentine's Day • *Get a Different Name Day • Man Day • World Radio Day

14. *ENAIC Computer Introduced (1946) • *Ferris Wheel Day • *First African American to be Recorded on Vinyl (1920) • *First Presidential Photograph (1849) • *League of Women Voters Formed (1920) • National Donor Day • Race Relations Day • *Saint Valentine's Day

15. *Susan B Anthony Birthday (1820) • *Asteroid Near Miss Day • *Canada: Maple Leaf Flag Adopted (1910) • *Chelyabinsky Meteor Explosion (2013) • *Galileo Galilei Birthday (1564) • Iceland: Bun Day • Love Reset Day • *Lupercalia, Remember the *Maine* Day (1898) • *Serbia: National Day

16. Lithuania: Independence Day

17. *League of United Latin American Citizens (LULAC) Founded (1927) • *My Way Day • *National PTA Founders' Day (1897)

18. Gambia: Independence Day • Nepal: National Democracy Day • George Peabody (1795) • *Pluto Discovery Day (1930)

19. *Japanese Internment (80th Anniversary, 1942) • *Knights of Pythias Founding (1864) • National Airboat Day • Skate Shop Day • *US Landing on Iwo Jima (1945) • World Pangolin Day

20. Ansel Adams Day (1902) • Closest Approach of a Comet to Earth (1491) • Daytona 500 • *Northern Hemisphere Hoodie-Hoo Day • *United Nations: World Day for Social Justice

21. Bangladesh: Martyrs Day • Canada: Family Day (selected provinces) • CIA Agent Arrested as Spy Day • Presidents' Day • *United Nations: International Mother Language Day • George Washington`s Birthday Observed • *Washington Monument Dedicated (1885)

22. Digital Learning Day • Montgomery Boycott Arrests (1956) • National Margarita Day • Saint Lucia: Independence Day • *George Washington's Birthday (1732) • Woolworth's Day (First Chain Store, 1879) • World Spay Day

23. Brunei Darussalam: National Day • *Curling is Cool Day • Diesel Engine Day • Guyana: Anniversary of Republic • George Handel Day (1685) *Iwo Jima Day (1945) • Japan: Birthday of the Emperor • Russia: Defender of the Fatherland Day • Single-Tasking Day

24. Estonia: Independence Day • Georgian Calendar Day • Introduce a Girl to Engineering Day (Discovere Girl Day) • Mexico: Flag Day • National Chili Day

25. Clay Becomes Heavyweight Champ (1964) • Kuwait: National Day

26. Carpe Diem Day • *FCC (Federal Communications Commission) created (1934) • *For Pete's Sake Day • Grand Canyon National Park Established (1919) • Kuwait: Liberation Day • Open that Bottle Night • *Levi Strauss Day • World Sword Swallowers Day • World Trade Center Bombing of 1993

27. Dominican Republic: Independence Day • Fasching Sunday • International Polar Bear Day • Henry Wadsworth Longfellow (1807) • Orthodox Meatfare Sunday • Shrovetide

28. Fasching • Floral Design Day • Iceland: Bun Day • *National Tooth Fairy Day • Shrove Monday • Taiwan: 288 Memorial Day

# Holiday Marketing Ideas

**National Time Management Month** — Step back and evaluate your use of your most valuable asset, your time. Taking the time to understand where you're spending your time wisely, and where you aren't, will give you a better handle on the way you manage your time.

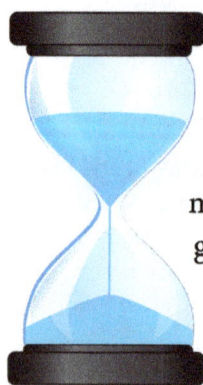

You need to know how to better manage your time with your customers while marketing your business. Offer branded tips and graphics on social media or better yet, gather a group of experts and sponsor or host a seminar or webinar.

Since this holiday encompasses the entirety of February, you can either schedule it once during the month or for as many days as you are up to handling. Maybe once a week for the entire month with only one speaker each day will work for you and your customers.

**Feb 10 WWII Medal of Honor Day** — This holiday is about celebrating our heroes. Think about who your heroes are. If they aren't your customers who keep you in business, then you are probably missing a terrific marketing opportunity today. Today is your chance to change that. Perhaps a discount could be offered to them.

Another fun thing to do might be to create your own branded 'medal of honor' badge and email it to your favorite, most loyal customers. Every chance you have to get your name in front of them helps to remind them that you are here for them when they or even their peeps need your business offerings. You'll find a sample in the appendix.

If you want to go big time, gather a group of like-minded business owners and either visit your local VA hospital and host an event, maybe a sing-along, or just sit and listen to them regale their stories. When you find a way to capture the media's attention you might even get some local exposure for you or your group!

**Feb 22 Digital Learning Day** — This holiday speaks for itself. Social media tips and graphics could be a good start, but to really make an impact host or sponsor an event! There is a plethora of things people want to learn and there's no reason why you shouldn't take advantage of the opportunity to share your knowledge and grow your business.

**Feb 26 For Pete's Sake Day** — This is a day when ladies and gents alike honor the time old tradition of not swearing in a lady's company. Instead, a 'minced oath' such as this one or, 'Oh sugar' and 'For crying out loud' are substituted.

I am thinking proper manners could be the subject of your marketing campaign today. I'm sure you would agree that today's youth need this instruction more now than ever. Therefore, branded graphics with tips on proper etiquette are the order de jour. Maybe a training class if you are up to the challenge. Remember, events are where it's at when it comes to marketing your wares.

# MARCH

Mar 1 – 14 Mardi Gras

Mar 2 – Apr 16 Lent

Mar 4 – 13 XIII Paralympic Winter Games, Beijing

Mar 5 – 20 Iditarod Trail Sled Dog Race

Mar 7 – Apr 15 Orthodox Lent

Mar 13 – Apr 15 Deaf History Month

## Month-Long Holidays

Alport Syndrome Awareness Month • American Red Cross Month • Brain Injury Awareness Month • Credit Education Month • Employee Spirit Month • Humorists are Artists Month (HAAM) • International Black Women in Jazz Month • International Ideas Month • International Mirth Month • Irish American Heritage Month • March Frozen Food Month • Music in Our Schools Month • National Clean Up Your IRS Act Month • National Colorectal Cancer Awareness Month • National Kidney Month • National Ladder Safety Month • National Multiple Sclerosis Education and Awareness Month • National Nutrition Month®, National Peanut Month • National Umbrella Month • National Women's History Month • Optimism Month • Paws to Read Month • Play-the-Recorder Month • Poison Prevention Awareness Month • Red Cross Month • Save the Vaquita Month • Save Your Vision Month • Social Work Month • Women's History Month • Workplace Eye Wellness Month • Worldwide Home Schooling Awareness Month • Youth Art Month

## Week-Long Holidays

Mar 1 – 7 National Cheerleading Week • National Invest in Veterans Week • Return the Borrowed Books Week • Will Eisner Week

Mar 5 – 6 National Day of Unplugging

Mar 6 – 12 Celebrate Your Name Week • Termite Awareness Week • Words Matter Week

Mar 7 – 11 National School Breakfast Week

Mar 14 – 20 Brain Awareness Week

Mar 19 – 20 Military Through the Ages

Mar 20 – 26 National Poison Prevention Week • National Protocol Officers Week • World Folk Tales and Fables Week

Mar 21 – 24 Italy: Bologna Children's Book Fair

Mar 21 – 27 International Teach Music Week • United Kingdom: Shakespeare Week • United Nations: Week of Solidarity with the Peoples Struggling Against Racism and Racial Discrimination

Mar 23 – 26 Association of Writers and Writing Programs Conference and Bookfair

# Daily Holidays

1. Baby Sleep Day • Bosnia and Herzegovina: Independence Day • Ralph Waldo Emerson Birthday (1914) • *Iceland: Beer Day & Bursting Day • Japan: Omizutori (Water-Drawing Festival) • Korea: Samiljol or Independence Movement Day • Land Mine Ban Day • National Horse Protection Day (World Horse Day) • National Pig Day • Paraguay: National Heroes' Day • Peace Corps Day • Plan a Solo Vacation Day • Refired, Not Retired Day • Shrove Tuesday • Switzerland: Chalandra Marz • Town Meeting Day • Wales: Saint David's Day • World Compliment Day • Zero Discrimination Day

2. Ash Wednesday • Ethiopia: Adwa Day • *Highway Numbers Day (1925) • *King Kong Day • NEA's Read Across America Day • Texas Independence Day

3. Alexander Graham Bell Birthday (1847) • *Bonza Bottler Day™ • Bulgaria: Liberation Day • Hin-Mah-Too-Yah-Lat-Kekt Birthday (1840) • International Ear Care Day • Japan: Hina Matsuri (Doll Festival) • Malawi: Martyr's Day • National Anthem Day • Simplify-Your-Life Day • United Kingdom and Ireland: World Book Day • United Nations: World Wildlife Day • What if Cats and Dogs Had Opposable Thumbs Day • World Birth Defects Day

4. Dress in Blue Day • National Backcountry Ski Day • *National Grammar Day • Old Inauguration Day • Shabbat Across America and Canada • World Day of Prayer • World Engineering Day for Sustainable Development

5. National Poutine Day • Saint Piran's Day

6. *Dred Scott day • Ghana: Independence Day • *Michelangelo (1475) • Namesake Day • Orthodox Cheesefare Sunday (Forgiveness Sunday)

7. Australia: Eight Hour Day or Labor Day • Fun Facts About Names Day • Guam: Discovery Day or Magellan Day • Orthodox Green Monday

8. International (Working) Women's Day • National Proofreading Day • Syrian Arab Republic: Revolution Day • Unique Names Day • United Nations: International Women's Day • United States Income Tax Anniversary (1913)

9. *Barbie Day • Belize: Baron Bliss Day • Discover What Your Name Means Day • Panic Day • Registered Dietitian Nutritionists Day

10. International Bagpipe Day • *Mario Day • Name Tag Day • National Women and Girls HIV/ AIDS Awareness Day • *Salvation Army in the US (1880) • *Telephone Invention (1876) • *US Paper Money Issued (1862) • World Kidney Day

11. Bureau of Indian Affairs Established (1824) • Dream 2022 Day • *Johnny Appleseed Day • Key Deer Awareness Day • Lithuania: Restitution of Independence Day • Middle Name Pride Day • WHO Declares COVID-19 Global Pandemic (2020)

12. *FDR's First Fireside Chat (1933) • Gabon: National Day • Genealogy Day • *Girl Scouts of the USA (1912) • Great Blizzard of '88 • International Fanny Pack Day • Lesotho: Moshoeshe's Day • Mauritius: Independence Day

13. Check Your Batteries Day • Daylight Savings Begins • *Earmuffs Day • Good Samaritan Involvement Day • Holy See: National Day • National Open an Umbrella Indoors Day • Planet Uranus Discovery Day (1781)

14. *Albert Einstein Birthday (1879) • Fill Our Staplers Day • International Day of Mathematics • Moth-er Day • National Napping Day • Pi Day • "10 Most Wanted List" Day (1950) • United Nations: Commonwealth Day

15. Belarus: Constitution Day • Brutus Day • Ides of March • International Day of Action for the Seals • Liberia: J.J. Roberts Day • National VO Day • True Confessions Day

16. *Black Press Day (1827) • Curlew Day • Freedom of Information Day • Goddard Day • *Lips Appreciation Day • National Panda Day • No Selfies Day • US Military Academy Founded (1802)

17. Absolutely Incredible Kid Day • *Campfire USA Day • Evacuation Day • Ireland: National Day • Saint Patrick's Day • Purim

18. Aruba: Flag Day • Diesel Day • Forgive Mom and Dad Day • India: Holi • *National Biodiesel Day

19. Certified Nurses Day • *Wyatt Earp (1848) • Iran: National Day of Oil • National Quilting Day • Play-the-Recorder Day • Saint Joseph's Day • Save the Florida Panther Day • Swallows Return to San Juan Capistrano Day • US Standard Time Act (1920)

20. Ostara • Proposal Day® (also Sept 22) • Tunisia: Independence Day • United Nations: French Language Day • *United Nations: International Day of Happiness • *Won't You Be My Neighbor Day

21. *Bach Day • England: Care Sunday • *First Round-the-World Balloon Flight (1999) • Iranian New Year: (Noruz) • Japan: Vernal Equinox Day • Lesotho: National Tree Planting Day • Memory Day • Namibia: Independence Day • National Healthy Fats Day • Naw-Ruz • South Africa: Human Rights Day • *Twitter Day • *United Nations: International Day for the Elimination of Racial Discrimination • United Nations: International Day of Forests • United Nations: International Nowruz Day • United Nations: World Poetry Day • World Down Syndrome Day

22. As Young As You Feel Day • India: New Year's Day • *International Day of The Seal • *Louis L'Amour Day (1908) • Laser Patented Day (1960) • National Agriculture Day,*National Goof-off Day • Puerto Rico: Emancipation Day • United Nations: World Day for Water (aka World Water Day)

23. "Big Bertha Paris Gun Day • *Liberty Day • National Puppy Day • National Tamale Day • *Near Miss Day • New Zealand: Otago and Southland Provincial Anniversary • "OK" Day • Pakistan: Republic Day • *United Nations: World Meteorological Day

24. Argentina: National Day of Memory for Truth and Justice • Exxon Valdez Oil Spill (1989) • *Houdini Day (1874) • Philippine Independence • *World Tuberculosis Day

25. *Bed In for Peace Day • *Greece: Independence Day • Maryland Day • National Medal of Honor Day • *Old New Year's Day • Pecan Day • Tolkien Reading Day • United Nations: International

Day of Remembrance of The Victims of Slavery and The Transatlantic Slave Trade • United Nations: International Day of Solidarity with Detained and Missing Staff Members

26. Bangladesh: Independence Day • Camp David Accord Day • Earth Hour • *Legal Assistants Day • Live Long and Prosper Day • *Make Up Your Own Holiday Day • Support Women Artists Now Day (SWAN Day) • Walk in the Sand Day

27. Alaska: Earthquake (1964) • England: Mothering Sunday • European Union: Daylight Saving Time (begins) • *FDA Approves Viagra Day • Myanmar: Resistance Day • *Quirky Country Music Song Titles Day

28. "Big Bang" Day • Czech Republic: Teachers' Day • Seward's Day

29. Canada: British North America Act (1867) • Central African Republic: Boganda Day • Dow Jones Day • Knights of Columbus Founder's Day • *Niagara Falls Runs Dry (1848) • Taiwan: Youth Day • Texas Loves Children Day

30. Anesthetic Day • *Doctors Day • Grass is Always Browner on the Other Side of the Fence Day • Little Red Wagon Day • Manatee Appreciation Day • *Pencil Day • Trinidad and Tobago: Spiritual/Shouter Baptist Liberation Day • Vincent Van Gogh Day (1853) • Whole Grains Sampling Day • World Bipolar Day

31. *Bunsen Burner Day • Cesar Chavez Day • *Eiffel Tower Day (1998) • International Hug a Medievalist Day • *National "She's Funny That Way" Day • US Virgin Islands: Transfer Day • World Back-up Day

# Holiday Marketing Ideas

**International Ideas Month**—Let your creativity flow. Whether you decide to create, join, or just participate in a mastermind class, this would be the proper time to do so. I have it on good authority that a mastermind group can be beneficial when you need a 'sounding board' to bounce your ideas around.

Another benefit is that the ebb and flow during the discussions can spark creative ideas to help you along your business' path to success.

**Mar 7 Fun Facts About Names Day**—Start off this weird & wacky holiday with fun facts about your own name. Then invite others to participate. If you can, try to uncover where your name originated, what country it is most used, and what is it's hidden meaning.

One sure way to market your business today is to send a note to each of your customers, or just your favorite, most loyal ones, with an explanation of what their name means. This is sure to endear you to them, give them a giggle, and remind them of your business. Keeping your customers and clients aware that you exist is always a good idea. Especially now that so many doors have closed due to the pandemic.

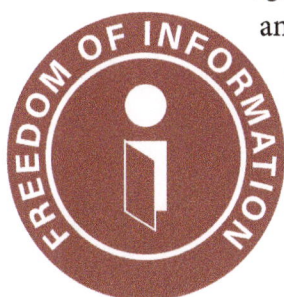

**Mar 16 Freedom of Information Day**—Gives you the opportunity to be open and honest with your customers. As a reminder, simply sharing what your business policies are that affect their personal information can do two beneficial things. Firstly, it will confirm with them your commitment to the security of

the information they have shared with you. Secondly, they will be reminded of you and your business. When they, or the people they come in contact with, need your products and services your business will be already in the minds and on the tip of their tongues.

As always, simple social media graphics will work when you brand them to your business.

**Mar 21 Memory Day** — Some fun things you can do today revolve around events. Gather a group and play some silly memory games. I have added a couple to the Samples Appendix for you to use.

As I have said before, events are an easy way to market your business, and when you make them fun your attendees will appreciate your organizational skills. Oh, did I just open the door for event planners here? *giggle*

**Mar 26 Make Up Your Own Holiday Day** — This one says it all! Any excuse will do. It's your chance to invent a weird & wacky holiday theme, possibly inspired by a current widely recognized public event, and develop a marketing plan around it. Whether that means simple graphics to share or something that takes prior preparation, this is totally up to you.

# APRIL

Apr 2 – May 1 Ramadan
Apr 3 – 16 Passiontide
Apr 26 – May 31 Adopt a Horse Month

## Month-Long Holidays

Adopt a Ferret Month • Alcohol Awareness Month • Autism Acceptance Month • Beaver Awareness Month • Couple Appreciation Month • Distracted Driving Awareness Month • Grange Month • Holy Humor Month • Informed Woman Month • International Black Women's History Month • International Customer Loyalty Month • International Twit Award Month • Jazz Appreciation Month • Mathematics and Statistics Awareness Month • Medical Cannabis Education and Awareness Month • National African American Women's Fitness Month • National Cancer Control Month • National Card and Letter Writing Month • National Child Abuse Prevention Month • National Donate Life Month • National Frog Month • National Heartworm Awareness Month • National Humor Month • National Knuckles Down Month • National Lawn Care Month • National 9-1-1 Education Month • National Pecan Month • National Poetry Month • National Rebuilding Month • National Sexual Assault Awareness and Prevention Month • Occupational Therapy Month • Pet First Aid Awareness Month • Prevention of Cruelty to Animals Month • Rosacea Awareness Month • School Library Month • Straw Hat Month • Stress Awareness Month • Women's Eye Health and Safety Month • Workplace Conflict Awareness Month • World Landscape Architecture Month • Worldwide Bereaved spouses Awareness Month • Youth Sports Safety Month

## Week-Long Holidays

Apr 1 – 7 Laugh at Work Week • Testicular Cancer Awareness Week
Apr 2 – 10 National Robotics Week
Apr 3 – 9 Consider Christianity Week • National Library Week • National Window Safety Week • Passion Week
Apr 4 – 9 Explore Your Career Options Week
Apr 4 – 10 Hate Week — "Down with Big Brother"
Apr 10 – 16 Greece: Dumb Week • Holy Week • National Dog Bite Prevention Week • Pan American Week • Philippines: Holy Week
Apr 16 – 22 Invictus Games — The Hague 2022
Apr167 – 24 National Park Week
Apr 16 – 23 Pesach or Passiontide

Apr 17 – 23 Chemists Celebrate Earth Week • National Coin Week • Orthodox Holy Week

Apr 23 – 24 Just Pray No! Worldwide Weekend of Prayer and Fasting

Apr 24 – 30 *National Crime Victims' Rights Week • National Pediatric Transplant Week • Preservation Week • Sky Awareness Week • World Immunization Week

# Daily Holidays

1. *April Fool's or All Fool's Day • Bulgaria: St Lasarus' Day • International Kids' Yoga Day • Iran: Islamic Republic Day • Library Snapshot Day • Mylesday • US Air Force Day

2. Hans Christian Anderson Day (1805) • Argentina: Malvinas Day • *Sir Alec Guinness (1914) • International Pillow Fight Day • National Ferret Day • Pascua Florida Day • Pharmacists in Public Health Day • Ponce de Leon Discovers Florida (1513) • *Reconciliation Day • *United Nations: World Autism Awareness Day • US Mint Day

3. Blacks Ruled Eligible to Vote Day (1944) • England: Care Sunday • Guinea: Anniversary of the Second Republic • *Pony Express Day • *Tweed Day

4. Maya Angelou Birthday (1928) • *Beatles Take Over Music Charts (1964) • *Bonza Bottler Day™ • Flag Act of 1818 Day • Senegal: Independence Day • Taiwan: Children's Day • *United Nations: International Day for Mine Awareness and Assistance in Mine Action • *Vitamin C Day

5. Gold Star Spouses Day • National Deep-Dish Pizza Day • National Library Workers Day

6. Drowsy Driver Awareness Day • National Library Outreach Day • North Pole Discovery Day • *Tartan Day • *Teflon Day (1938) • Thailand: Chakri Day • Twinkies Day • United Nations: International Day of Sport for Development and Peace

7. *International Beaver Day • International Snail-papers Day • *Metric System Day • National Beer Day (1933) • National Making the First Move Day • *No Housework Day • Rwanda: Genocide Remembrance Day • Switzerland: Näfels Pilgrimage • Take Action for Libraries Day • United Nations: International Day of the Reflection on the Genocide in Rwanda • *United Nations: World Health Day • WHO Day

8. Home Run Record Set by Hank Aaron (1974) • International Roma Day • Japan: Flower Festival (Hana Matsuri) • National Dog Fighting Awareness Day

9. *Civil Rights Bill of 1866 Day • Civil War Ends (1865) • Denmark: Flag Day • *Jenkins Ear Day • Jumbo the Elephant Day • National Former Prisoner of War Recognition Day • Philippines: Araw Ng Kagitingan • Texas Panhandle Tornado Day • Tunisia: Martyrs' Day • *Winston Churchill Day

10. ASPCA Incorporation Day (1866) • *Commodore Perry Day • First Image of a Black Hole Day (2019) • Ireland: Good Friday Peace Agreement in Northern Ireland (1998) • *National Siblings Day (World Siblings Day) • Palm Sunday • *Salvation Army Founder's Day

11. *Barbershop Quartet Day • Civil Rights Act Day (1968) • Costa Rica: Juan Santamaria Day • *International "Louie Louie" Day • National Clean Up Your Pantry Day • National Pet Day • Uganda: Liberation Day • World Parkinson's Day

12. Children's Day in Florida (always the second Tuesday) • Education and Sharing Day • Halifax: Independence Day • International Be Kind to Lawyers Day,*National D.E.A.R. Day (aka Drop

Everything and Read) • *National Licorice Day • Polio Vaccine Day • Truancy Day • United Nations: International Day of Human Space Flight • *Walk on Your Wild Side Day • Yuri's Night

13. *Guy Fawkes Day • *Thomas Jefferson Day • National Signing Day—College Basketball • Sri Lanka: Sinhala and Tamil New Year

14. *Children with Alopecia Day • Dictionary Day • Honduras: Dia de las Americas • India: Mahavir Jayanti & Vaisakhi • *International Moment of Laughter Day • Maundy Thursday or Holy Thursday • National Pecan Day • Pan American Day • Pathologists' Assistant Day • World Chagas Day

15. Astronomers Find New Solar System (1999) • Bermuda: Good Friday Kite Flying Day • Boston Marathon and Bombing (2013) • Botox Day • Emancipation Day (observed) • First School for Deaf Founded (1817) • Good Friday • *Income Tax Pay Day • *McDonald's Day • *National Take a Wild Guess Day • *National That Sucks Day • Quarterly Estimated Federal Income Tax Payers' Due Date (also Jan 17, Jun 15, and Sep 15, 2022) • *Titanic Sinking (1912) • World Art Day

16. *Charlie Chaplin Day (1889) • Easter Even • Emancipation Day • Lazarus Sunday • National Stress Awareness Day • World Circus Day

17. American Samoa: Flag Day • *Blah! Blah! Blah! Day • Easter Sunday • International Haiku Poetry Day • Orthodox Palm Sunday • Poland: Solidarity Granted Legal Status (1989) • Syrian Arab Republic: Independence Day

18. Boston Marathon (126th Running) • Canada: Constitution Act of 1982 • Dyngus Day • Easter Monday • Paul Revere's Ride Day (1775) • *Pet Owners Independence Day • South Africa: Family Day • "Third World" Day • World Heritage Day/International Day for Monuments and Sites • Zimbabwe: Independence Day

19. John Parker Day • National Hanging Out Day • Patriots Day in Florida • Sierra Leone: National Holiday • Swaziland: King's Birthday • Uruguay: Landing of the 33 Patriots Day

20. 4/20 Day • United Nations: Chinese Language Day

21. Aggie Muster Day • Brazil: Tiradentes Day • Get to Know Your Customers Day (third Thursday of each quarter is set aside to get to know your customers even better) • Iceland: First Day of Summer • Indonesia: Kartini Day • Italy: Birthday of Rome • *Kindergarten Day • National Bulldogs are Beautiful Day • National High Five Day • Red Baron Day • San Jacinto Day • United Nations: World Creativity and Innovation Day

22. Brazil: Discovery of Brazil Day • Coins Stamped "In God We Trust" Day • *Earth Day • *National Jelly Bean Day • Oklahoma Land Rush Day (1889) • United Nations: International Mother Earth Day

23. Canada: Newfoundland: Saint George's Day • *Movie Theatre Day • *Public School Day • National English Muffin Day • Pet Tech CPR Day® • Physicists Discover Top Quark (1994) • Record Store Day • Saint George Feast Day • William Shakespeare Day (1564) • Spain: Book Day and Lover's Day • Turkey: National Sovereignty and Children's Day • United Nations: English Language Day • United Nations: Spanish Language Day • *United Nations: World Book and Copyright Day • World Book Night

24. Armenia: Armenian Martyrs Day • Independent Bookstore Day • Ireland: Easter Rising (1916) • Library of Congress Day • Easter Sunday or Pascha • Switzerland: Landsgemeinde

25. Abortion Legalized (1967) • Anzac Day • Egypt: Sinai Day • *License Plates Day • Italy: Liberation Day • Portugal: Liberty Day • Swaziland: National Flag Day • World Malaria Day • World Penguin Day • WWII: East Meets West Day (1945)

26. Audubon Day • *Hug an Australian Day • National Help a Horse Day • National Pretzel Day • *Richter Scale Day • Tanzania: Union Day • United Nations: International Chernobyl Disaster Remembrance Day • United Nations: World Intellectual Property Day

27. Administrative Professionals Day or Secretary's Day • Babe Ruth Day (1947) • Mantanzas Mule Day • *Morse Code Day • Most Tornadoes in a Day (US) • National Little Pampered Dog Day • Netherlands: King's Day • Sierra Leon and Togo: Independence Day • Slovenia: Insurrection Day • South Africa: Freedom Day

28. Biological Clock Gene Discovered (1994) • Canada: National Day of Mourning • Israel: Yom Hashoah • National Teach Children to Save Day • Take Our Daughters and Sons to Work® Day (fourth Thursday in April) • United Nations: World Day for Safety and Health at Work • Workers Memorial Day

29. Arbor Day in Arizona • Emperor Hirohito Michi-No-Miya Birthday (1901) • Japan: Showa Day • National Arbor Day • National Hairball Awareness Day • *"Peace" Rose Day • Zipper Day (1913)

30. Beltane • *Bugs Bunny Day (1938) • Día de los Niños/Día de los Libros • First North America Theatrical Performance Day (1598) • Independent Bookstore Day • International Jazz Day • Louisiana Purchase Day (1803) • National Animal Advocacy Day • National Honesty Day (Honest Abe Awards) • Raisin Day • National Rebuilding Day • Organization of American States Founded (1948) • Solar Eclipse • Vietnam: Liberation Day • *Walpurgis Night • World Healing Day • World Tai Chi and Qigong Day • World Veterinary Day

# Holiday Marketing Ideas

**Apr Holy Humor Month** —Share some of your favorite jokes this month but be sure to keep them clean enough that little eyes and ears can enjoy them as well. A few of my favorites can be found in the appendix.

A giggle a day that you brand to your business is a sure way to capture the hearts and attention of your potential customers and clients. After all, this entire *Weird & Wacky Holiday Marketing Guide* is all about keeping your marketing fun and effective.

**Apr 3 Tweed Day** — It's not hard to imagine what this weird & wacky holiday celebrates. However, it's not just about the fabric, it's about a notorious criminal named William "Boss" Tweed.

Nevertheless, besides wearing tweed, you might consider the famous Sherlock Holmes, who exemplifies tweed. Have some fun by imitating the character with his dress, his mannerisms, and his famous quotes. It's elementary, my dear Watson.

On social media be sure to use the hashtag #National Tweed Day.

**Apr 9 Jumbo the Elephant Day** —Think humongous! Put your best marketing plan in action today and generate ginormous profits. While a deep discount on products and services is always noteworthy to your customers, extra bonuses might be an alternative to the sales price drop. Consider both and then put on an event to showcase your Jumbo the Elephant Day Holiday Sales Event.

When you work with other retailers to get the word out and share the huge marketing event, you can multiply your efforts tenfold.

If you want to do something a little less time consuming, there's always the social media to fall back on. But wouldn't a notecard wishing your customers a happy JE Day be a better course of action?

**Apr 14 Dictionary Day** — This could be a super fun day to celebrate while promoting your business. While searching the web my editor noticed a website that I couldn't resist including. The link to it can be found in the appropriate appendix. It is "Merriam-Webster's Great Big List of Beautiful and Useless Words, Vol. 3". Now that's pretty darn weird & wacky, wouldn't you say? So, why not use some of the words on that site as you post on social media today? Better yet, create an infographic, or a simple branded graphic, to show your own weird & wacky side.

**Apr 15 Botox Day** — Today's weird & wacky holiday fills me with marketing ideas. Filling in the gaps in your business such as expanding your offerings, smoothing out the wrinkles in your communication skills, and expanding your marketing plan. All of these ideas could easily be addressed in either a mastermind group or event. Don't know how to set-up a mastermind group of your own? You'll find the instructions in the appendix.

Helping others put their best face forward should be the goal for your marketing plan of the day. Could that mean sharing how to dress for success? What about a makeup party if you are a beauty consultant? Anything that might help your customers and clients is always a fulfilling venture.

When you can showcase your business through cross-promotions, events, and training the end results will cause your business to shine in the eyes of your customers and clients.

At the very least, you could rely on social media graphics. Lest you forget, #botoxday is your hashtag of the day.

**Apr 27 Most Tornadoes in a Day Day** — It's a whirlwind of an opportunity to stir up the sales today. Whipping together an event that creates a frenzy of activity in your business is what this day is about.

Consider creating a storm by offering a funnel of offerings. The more they buy, the bigger the discount, or maybe offer a deal that if they purchase a specific item, they'll get another item free. Like a two fer, but not of the same item. That way, you can introduce them to something they may not have tried before. If they like it, perhaps they'll buy it from you in the future.

# MAY

May 1 – 31 Philippines: Santacruzan
May 30 – Sep 5 National Marina Days

## Month-Long Holidays

American Cheese Month • Asian American and Pacific Islander Heritage Month • Asthma Awareness Month • Celiac Disease Awareness Month • Clap 4 Health Month • College Students with Disabilities Recognition Month • Gardening for Wildlife Month • Gifts from the Garden Month • Haitian Heritage Month • Heal the Children Month • Huntington's Disease Awareness Month • International Mediterranean Diet Month • International Victorious Woman Month • Jewish American Heritage Month • Mental Health Month • Motorcycle Safety Month • National Allergy/Asthma Awareness Month • National Arthritis Awareness Month • National Barbecue Month • National Bike Month • National Good Car-Keeping Month • National Hamburger Month • National Hepatitis Awareness Month • National Meditation Month • National Military Appreciation Month • National Osteoporosis Month • National Physical Fitness and Sports Month • National Read to Your Baby Bump Month • Older Americans Month • REACT Month • Save Your Tooth Month • Skin Cancer Awareness Month • Spiritual Literacy Month • Ultraviolet Awareness Month • Women's Health Care Month • Young Achievers Month

## Week-Long Holidays

May 1 – 7 Be Kind to Animals Week® • Choose Privacy Week • National Family Week • National Hug Holiday Week • National Pet Week • Update Your References Week

May 6 – 12 National Nurses Week

May 8 – 14 National Police Week • Salute to 35+ Moms Week • Tick Awareness Week • Work at Home Moms Week

May 9 – 13 National Etiquette Week • National Stuttering Awareness Week

May 15 – 21 International New Friends Old Friends Week • National Transportation Week National • Unicycle Week • Police Week • World Trade Week

May 19 – 22 Monaco: Grand Prix de Monaco

May 20 – 21 Fishing Has No Boundaries Days

May 21 – 27 National Safe Boating Week

May 29 – Jun 5 National African Violet Week

# Daily Holidays

1. *Amtrak • Batman Debut Anniversary (1939) • Great Britain Formed Day (1707) • Hug Your Cat Day • Japan: Reiwa Era Begins • Labor Day • *Law Day • *Lei Day • *Loyalty Day • *May Day • May One Day • Mother Goose Day • National Bubba Day • National Infertility Survival® Day • *New Home Owners Day • Russia: International Labor Day • *School Principals' Day

2. Ireland: May Day • King James Bible Published Day • Labor Day Observed • Melanoma Monday • Red Baron Day • Robert's Rules Day • United Nations: World Tuna Day

3. *Garden Meditation Day • Japan: Constitution Memorial Day • *Lumpy Rug Day • Mexico: Day of the Holy Cross • National Public Radio Day • National Specially Abled Pets Day • National Teacher Day • *National Two Different Colored Shoes Day • Poland: Constitution Day (Swieto Trzeciego Maja) • *United Nations: World Press Freedom Day

4. China: Youth Day • Curaçao: Memorial Day • Israel: Remembrance Day • Japan: Greenery Day • National Bike to School Day • Rhode Island: Independence Day • *Star Wars Day

5. African World Heritage Day • AMA Founded Day (1847) • *Bonza Bottler Day™ • *Cartoonists Day • *Cinco de Mayo • Ethiopia: Patriots Victory Day • International Day of the Midwife • Japan and South Korea: Children's Day • National Day of Prayer • National Day of Reason • Netherlands: Liberation Day • World Asthma Day • World Portuguese Language Day

6. International Management Accounting Day® • *Joseph Brackett Day • Military Spouse Appreciation Day *No Diet Day • *No Homework Day • Orson Wells Day (1915)

7. Beaufort Scale Day • Cystinosis Awareness Day • El Salvador: Day of the Soldier • England: Heston Furry dance/Flora Day • Free Comic Book Day • Germany Hamburg Harbor Day • Kentucky Derby • Learn to Ride a Bike Day • National Auctioneers Day • National Train Day • Spring Astronomy Day

8. China: Birth of Lord Buddha • Czech Republic: Liberation Day • France: Victory Day • Mother's Day • Mother's at the Wall Day • *No Socks Day • Slovakia: Liberation Day • *United Nations: Time of Remembrance and Reconciliation WWII (8–9) • *V E Day (1945) • *World Red Cross Red Crescent Day

9. European Union Founded (1950) • Russia: Victory Day • Uzbekistan: Day or Memory and Honor

10. Golden Spike Driving Day (1758) • Micronesia: Constitution Day • United Nations: International Day of Argania • World Lupus Day

11. Salvador Dali Day • Donate a Day's Wages to Charity Day • *Eat What You Want Day • National Nightshift Workers Day • National Receptionists Day • National School Nurse Day • National Third Shift Workers Day

12. *Limerick Day • Native American Rights Recognized Anniversary (1879) • Florence Nightingale Day • *Odometer Day

13. Blame Someone Else Day • Denmark: Common Prayer Day • Electric Razor Day • Friday the Thirteenth • National Hummus Day,*Peace Officer Memorial Day

14. Fahrenheit Day • International World Migratory Bird Day • Letter Carriers' "Stamp Out Hunger" Food Drive,*Lewis and Clark Expedition Sets Out Day (1804) • Netherlands: National Windmill Day • Smallpox Vaccine Discovery (1796) • Stay Up All Night Night • *The Stars and Stripes

Forever Day • *Underground America Day • United Nations: World Migratory Bird Day • WAAC Day (1942) • World Fair Trade Day

15. Flight Attendant Day • Japan: Aoi Matsuri (Hollyhock Festival) • Mexico: San Isidro Day • Nakba Day • National Sliders Day • *Nylon Stockings Day • Paraguay: Independence Day • Peace Officer Memorial Day • Ride a Unicycle Day • *United Nations: International Day of Families

16. *Biographer's Day • Birthday of the Buddha • First Woman to Climb Mt. Everest Day (1975) • International Day of Light • Luna Eclipse • Peabody Day

17. Brown vs. Board of Education (1954) • *First Kentucky Derby Day (1875) • *Same-Sex Marriages Day (2004) • Norway: Constitution Day • *United Nations: World Telecommunications and Information Society Day

18. Haiti: Flag and University Day • *International Museum Day • Turkmenistan: Revival and Unity Day • Uruguay: Battle of Las Piedras Day • *Visit Your Relatives Day

19. *Boys Club Day • Dark Day in New England • Hepatitis Testing Day • Ho Chi Minh Birthday (1890) • Lag B'Omer • Turkey: Youth and Sports Day

20. *Amelia Earhart Atlantic Crossing Day (1932) • Cameroon: National Holiday • East Timor: Anniversary of Independence • *Eliza Doolittle Day • Endangered Species Day • International Virtual Assistants Day • Lindbergh Flight (1927) • Mecklenburg Day • National Bike to Work Day • National Defense Transportation Day • National Pizza Party Day • Teacher's Day in Florida • United Nations: World Bee Day • *Weights and Measures Day • World Arthritis Day

21. *American Red Cross Founder's Day • Armed Forces Day • Chile: Battle of Iquique Day • *I Need a Patch for That Day • *National Wait Staff Day • Preakness Stakes • United Nations: International Tea Day • *United Nations: World Day for Cultural Diversity for Dialogue and Development

22. *National Maritime Day • Sri Lanka: National Heroes Day • Rogation Sunday • Rural Life Sunday • Sri Lanka: National Heroes Day • *United Nations: International Day for Biological Diversity • US Colored Troops Founders Day • World Goth Day • Yemen: National Day

23. *Bonnie and Clyde Death (1934) • Canada: Victory Day • *International World Turtle Day® • Morocco: National Day • National Best Friend-In-Law Day • New York Public Library Day • Sweden: Linnaeus Day • United Nations: International Day to End Obstetric Fistula

24. Belize: Commonwealth Day • Brooklyn Bridge Open (1883) • *Brother's Day • Bulgaria: Culture Day • Declaration of the Bab • Eritrea: Independence Day • International Tiara Day • *Morse Code Day • Queen Victory Day

25. African Freedom Day • Argentina: Revolution Day • *Ralph Waldo Emerson Birthday (1803) • *Greatest Day in Track and Field: Jessie Owens' Day • Jordan: Independence Day • *National Missing Children's Day • *National Tap Dance Day • Poetry Day in Florida • *Towel Day • United Nations: Week of Solidarity with Peoples of Non-Self-Governing Territories • World Otter Day

26. Ascension Day • Australia: Sorry Day • Georgia: Independence Day • John Wayne (1907) • World Lindy Hop Day

27. First Flight into the Stratosphere (1931) • First Running of the Preakness • *Golden Gate Bridge Day (1937)

28. *Amnesty International Founded (1961) • Azerbaijan: Day of the Republic • Ethiopia and Nepal: National Day • *Sierra Club Day (1892) • *Slugs Return from Capistrano Day

29. *Amnesty for Southern Rebels Day • Ascension of Baha'u'llah • Haiti: Mother's Day • Indianapolis 500-Mile Race • Israel: Jerusalem Day (Yom Yerushalayim) • *Mount Everest Summit Reached (1953) • National Alligator Day • *United Nations: International Day of United Nations Peacekeepers

30. Fabergé Day • *First American Daily Newspaper Published (1783) • *Loomis Day • Memorial Day (Traditional) • Prayer for Peace Memorial Day • Trinidad and Tobago: Indian Arrival Day

31. *Copyright Law Passed (1970) • Johnstown Flood Day • *United Nations: World No–Tobacco Day • *What You Think Upon Grows Day • *Walt Whitman Day

# Holiday Marketing Ideas

**Gardening for Wildlife Month**—This month it's an easy marketing idea for you. Simply take a packet of seeds and either attach your business card to it or create a branded seed packet cover for them. Then, get out there and hand them out. It's that simple. You have a whole month to get do this, so decide where you want to go and how often you want to do it. If your budget doesn't allow you to do it every day, then maybe a bag of seeds rather than individual seed packet is the way to go for you. Simply put the seeds in a small paper or plastic bag with instructions and staple your business card to them. That's one way to stay on budget while marketing your business in a way that others will appreciate.

**May 3 National Teachers Day**—Hats off to our teachers! In celebration of teachers everywhere, adults, children, gifted, and special ed; Olympic, sports, business, and career; religious, art, music, and beauty, all these teachers and more should be the focus of the day.

More often than not, teachers have to purchase supplies for their students using their own meager salaries. This can be problematic for them. To alleviate this situation, consider a funding drive with donations of school supplies going to a deserving school. This can be accomplished in a similar way to the Charity Fundraising Drive instructions in the appendix. The main difference is you will be contacting the school administration rather than a company. Each school has different needs and requirements. So, be sure to check with the school(s) of your choice.

Alternatively, you might join a group of your local businesses to put together a gift pack either for one especially deserving teacher or smaller gifts for all the teachers in one less affluent school.

If you do either of the previously mentioned projects, I highly recommend you contact your local media and let them know what you are doing. The press is always looking for 'feel good' stories to air. And we all know what a little press can do for your business!

In the 2012 edition of the Weird & Wacky Holiday Marketing Guide you will find several helpful press release and additional ideas provided by the National Educational Association (NEA).

**May 8 *No Socks Day** — Wiggle those piggies and flaunt that pedicure. Take a day at the beach or your downtown and organize a coastal or city 'clean-up'. With a nod to your media, your efforts will be richly rewarded.

One additional idea in the event category that was listed in the 2020 edition of the Weird & Wacky Holiday Marketing Guide is to organize a clothing drive for the benefit of school age children whose parents are unable to provide new clothes for them for school. Socks, underwear, and more are always well appreciated by the receiving child and helps to boost their self-esteem. Since the flyer I designed in the 2020 edition is dated as such, I have updated it and shared it in the appendix.

If you aren't in the mood to participate or sponsor something on such a grand style, then you could always post on social media. Tips on the health benefits of proper foot care would be appropriate, especially if you are a podiatrist or have feet related products to sell. Be sure to use the hashtags #NoSocksDay, #NoSocks, #barefoot, #may8th and see what others are doing to celebrate. I have shared a graphic in the appendix to get you started.

**May 13 Friday the Thirteenth** — Rather than hiding in fear of Friday the Thirteenth, poke your head out and celebrate this infrequent holiday. Did you know that every year there could be anywhere from one to three occurrences? This year, however, there is only one, today.

One way to acknowledge this weird & wacky holiday is to share facts about this day as tweets or graphics on social media. I discovered a few that I have placed in the appendix for your use.

**May 20 Eliza Doolittle Day** — Today we are reminded of the importance of speaking our native languages properly. In doing so, we honor our ancestors. To celebrate this holiday, you might want to share grammar or spelling tips on your favorite social media platforms.

Alternatively, you could attempt to teach others your native language or begin a new language course yourself. Proper diction and sentence structure can be learned and will aid you in building your communication skills.

If you work with children or adults who will be, or are, searching for a job, you could offer to go to your local public, private, or adult education center and speak on this important subject.

# JUNE

## Month-Long Holidays

Adopt-A-Shelter-Cat Month • African American Music Appreciation Month • Alzheimer's and Brain Awareness Month • Audiobook Appreciation Month • Canada: National Indigenous History Month • Cancer from the Sun Month • Caribbean American Heritage Month • Cataract Awareness Month • Dementia Care Professionals Month • Effective Communications Month • Entrepreneurs "Do It Yourself" Marketing Month • Gay and Lesbian Pride Month • Great Outdoors Month • International Men's Month • International Surf Music Month • June Dairy Month • Lesbian, Gay, Bisexual, Transgender and Queer Pride Month • Men's Health Education and Awareness Month • Migraine and Headache Awareness Month • National Aphasia Awareness Month • National Bathroom Reading Month • National Candy Month • National Caribbean American Heritage Month • National Foster a Pet Month • National Iced Tea Month • National Ocean Month • National Pollinator Month • National Rivers Month • National Rose Month • National Safety Month • National Soul Food Month • National Zoo and Aquarium Month • Outdoor Marketing Month • Perennial Gardening Month • PTSD Awareness Month • Rainbow Book Month™ • Rebuild Your Life Month • Skyscraper Month • Student Safety Month • World Roller Coaster Appreciation Month

## Week-Long Holidays

Jun 4 – 11 International Clothesline Week

Jun 5 – 11 Bed Bug Awareness Week • National Business Etiquette Week

Jun 12 – 18 National Flag Week

Jun 13 – 19 Meet a Mate Week

Jun 13 – 20 National Hermit Week

Jun 16 – 19 US Open

Jun 19 – 25 Greencare for Troops Awareness Week • Lightning Safety Awareness Week

Jun 20 – 26 United Kingdom: Insect Week

Jun 23 – 26 US Senior Open

Jun 25 – 26 ARRL Field Day

# Daily Holidays

1. Baby Boomers Recognition Day • China: International Children's Day • Global Running Day • *Heimlich Maneuver Day • Kenya Madaraka Day • Samoa: Independence Day • Say Something Nice Day • Superman Day • United Nations: Global Day of Parents

2. Bhutan: Coronation Day • Bhutan & United Kingdom: Coronation Day • Italy: Republic Day • Orthodox Ascension Day • Saint Erasmus Day • *Yell Fudge at the Cobras in North America Day (Don't laugh, I haven't seen any lately!)

3. Bahamas: Labor Day • *Chimborazo Day • Korea: Tano Day • National Donut Day • United Nations: World Bicycle Day • Zoot Suit Riots Anniversary (1943)

4. China: Tiananmen Square Massacre (1989) • Finland: Flag Day • First Free Flight by a Woman (1784) • National Trails Day • Pulitzer Prize Day (1917) • Shavout (begins at sundown) • Tonga: Emancipation Day • *United Nations: International Day of Innocent Children Victims of Aggression Day

5. *AIDS First Noted (1981) • *Apple II (1977) • Belmont Stakes • Celebration of the Arts Day • Denmark: Constitution Day • First Balloon Flight (1783) • HIV Long-term Survivors Awareness Day • Iran: Fifteenth of Khordad • National Cancer Survivors Day • Pentecost • *United Nations: International Day for the Fight Against Illegal • Unreported and Unregulated Fishing • United Nations: World Environment Day • Whitsunday

6. *Bonza Bottler Day™,*D–Day (1944) • England: Dicing for Bibles Day • *Drive in Movie Day (1933) • Japan: Day of the Rice God • Korea: Memorial Day • National Yo-Yo Day • Prop 13 Day (1978) • *SEC Day (1934) • Sweden: National Day • United Nations: Russian Language Day • Whitmonday • YMCA Day

7. *(Daniel) Boone Day • Germany: Waldchestag (Forest Day) • Mackintosh Day • Malta: National Day • Supreme Court Strikes Down Connecticut Law Banning Contraception (1965) • United Nations: World Food Safety Day

8. *United Nations: World Ocean Day • *Upsy Daisy Day • World Oceans Day

9. *Donald Duck Day • International Archives Day • Jordan: Accession Day

10. *AA Day (1935) • Congo: Brazzaville (Day of National Reconciliation) • Jordan: Great Arab Revolt and Army Day • National Ballpoint Pen Day • National Iced Tea Day • Portugal: Day of Portugal • US Mint Day

11. Belmont Stakes • Jacques Cousteau (1910) • *King Kamehameha Day (First Hawaiian King) • Libya: Evacuation Day • National Cotton Candy Day

12. *Baseball's First Perfect Game (1880) • Children's Day in Massachusetts • Children's Sunday • First Man-Powered Flight Across English Channel (1979) • Loving v. Virginia Day (1967) • Orlando Nightclub Massacre (2016) • Orthodox Pentecost • Paraguay: Peace with Bolivia Day • Philippines: Independence Day • Race Unity Day • Russia: Russia Day • *"Tear Down This Wall" Day • Trinity Sunday • United Nations: World Day Against Child Labor

13. Outdoor Marketing Day • United Nations: International Albinism Awareness Day

14. Alzheimer Day • Family History Day • First Nonstop Transatlantic Flight (1919) • First US Breach of Promise Day • *Flag Day • Japan: Rice Planting Festival • Malawi: Freedom Day • UNIVAC Computer Day • US Army Day • World Blood Donor Day

15. *Magna Carta Day (1215) • National Prune Day • Native American Citizenship Day • *Nature Photography Day • Quarterly Estimated Federal Income Tax Payers' Due Date (also Jan 17, Apr 15, and Sep 15, 2022) • United Nations: World Elder Abuse Awareness Day

16. *Bloomsday • Corpus Christi • First Roller Coaster Opens Day (1884) • House Divided Speech (1858) • *Ladies' Day (Baseball) • Recess at Work Day • South Africa: Youth Day • US Open

17. Bunker Hill Day • Iceland: Independence Day • South Africa Repeals Last Apartheid Law (1991) • *United Nations: World Day to Combat Desertification and Drought

18. Battle of Waterloo Day • Egypt: Evacuation Day • Longest Dam Race Day • Seychelles: Constitution Day • United Nations: Sustainable Gastronomy Day • World Juggling Day

19. Corpus Christi Observed • Father's Day • Lou Gehrig Day • *Juneteenth • Texas: Emancipation Day • United Nations: International Day for the Elimination of Sexual Violence in Conflict • Uruguay: Artigas Day • "War is Hell" Day (1879) • *World Sauntering Day

20. Argentina: Flag Day • Father's Day • *First Doctor of Science Earned by a Woman Day (1895) • *United Nations: World Refugee Day

21. Anne and Samantha Day • Canada: National Indigenous Peoples Day • Go Skateboarding Day • Greenland: National Holiday • Midsummer Day/Eve • National Energy Shopping Day • United Nations: International Day of Yoga • World Music Day/Fête de la Musique

22. Croatia: Antifascist Struggle Day • International Day or Radiant Peace • Malta: Mnarja • Stupid Guy Thing Day • United Kingdom: National Windrush Day • US Department of Justice (1870)

23. Estonia: Victory Day • *Let It Go Day • Luxembourg: National Holiday • Runner's Selfie Day • United Nations: International Widows Day • United Nations: Public Service Day

24. Canada: Saint John the Baptiste Day • *Celebration of the Senses Day • China: Macau Day • "Flying Saucer" Day • Latvia: John's Day • National Food Truck Day • Take Your Dog to Work Day® • Peru: Countryman's Day • Saint John the Baptist Day • Venezuela: Battle of Carabobo Day

25. Bhutan: National Day • Korea: Tano Day • Mozambique: Independence Day • Slovenia: National Day • Supreme Court Ruling Day (Bans School Prayer • Upholds Right to Die • United Nations: Day of the Seafarer

26. *Barcode Day • CN Tower Day (1976) • Federal Credit Union Act (1934) • Human Genome Mapped (2000) • Madagascar: Independence Day • Saint Lawrence Seaway Dedication (1959) • Supreme Court Strikes Down Defense of Marriage Act (2013) • United Nations Charter Signing (1945) • *United Nations: International Day Against Drug Abuse and Illicit Trafficking • *United Nations: International Day in Support of Victims of Torture

27. Canada: Discover Day (Newfoundland and Labrador) • *Decide to be Married Day • Djibouti: Independence Day • *Happy Birthday to "Happy Birthday to You" Day • Industrial Workers of the World Day • *National HIV Testing Day • PTSD Awareness Day • United Nations: Micro-, Small-, and Medium-Sized Enterprises Day

28. International Lightning Safety Day • Monday Holiday Law (1968) • National Columnists' Day • Treaty of Versailles (1919)

29. *Death Penalty Ban Day • Interstate Highway System Born (1956) • Saint Peter and Paul Day • Saint Peter's Day • Seychelles: Independence Day • United Nations: International Day of the Tropics

30. Asteroid Day • Britain Cedes Claim to Hong Kong (1997) • Charles Blondin's Conquest of Niagara Falls (1859) • Congo: Independence Day • Gone with the Wind Published (1936) • Guatemala: Armed Forces Day • *Leap Second Adjustment Time Day • National Handshake Day • *NOW (National Organization of Women) Founded (1966) • Sudan: Revolution Day

# Holiday Marketing Ideas

**National Candy Month** —If you are a lover of everything sweet, as I am, you'll enjoy this super month-long weird & wacky holiday. While this celebration may indulge the senses of those who sell sweet confections, they are far from the only ones who can benefit from focusing their marketing efforts on this tantalizing holiday.

Sharing candy recipes that you have branded to your business, sending a sweet treat to your most loyal customers, and even handing out individually wrapped candies with either your branded wrapper or business card attached are all scrumptious ideas. If you recall, there is a mini-candy wrapper template that you can freely use and share in the appendix.

If you opt for sending candy to your best customers and clients, may I suggest you either support a small business or See's Candies for an extra-special treat for your mouthwatering purchases. You'll find See's Candies link in the appropriate appendix.

**Jun 6 National Yo-Yo Day**—Just for fun why not share videos on social media training how to do tricks with Yo-Yos? If you can do them yourself, so much the better.

However, you also have the option of hosting an event that is focused on some aspect of Yo-Yoing. A few that I can suggest are learning how to overcome the Yo-Yo diet syndrome, how to break the thread of a bad habit that is keeping your customers and clients from accomplishing their goals, or perhaps teaching others how to swing around the common mistakes that threaten to stop the pendulum of success in their lives and businesses.

For the faint of heart there's always social media graphics or tips that can be shared on these and more Yo-Yo themed subjects. Add a hashtag #YoYo to your posts to see what others are doing to celebrate this tricky day.

**Jun 13 Outdoor Marketing Day**—This holiday speaks for itself. Get out there and market your business. I know getting out of your comfort zone can be a daunting task in and of itself. But today is the day you should make your mark. Whether that means participating in an event or merely starting up a conversation with those you come in contact with, or even handing out your business card every chance you get, today is the day to get it done.

A simple task for you to accomplish today would be to find as many job, or services cork boards that you can pin your business card, or a simple discount offer on. Often, you'll find these in health food stores and community recreation areas to get you started.

**Jun 24 "Flying Saucer" Day** — Frisbees and sandwiches filled with Sloppy Joe mix and cheese. What do these two things have in common? They are both 'flying saucers'. While I must admit, they are vastly different, they both can be fun to toss around today.

As with Yo-Yo day, Frisbee throwing has its own set of tricks that you can teach and share. If you want to make it an event that the media will take notice of, consider gathering a group of children from your neighborhood. Show them ways that they can fling their 'flying saucers' that will give them something other than getting in trouble to do in their free time.

If you sponsor the event, you might even consider branding the Frisbees and giving each child one to take home. Oh, and be sure to serve Hawaiian Flying Saucers for lunch. The instructions on how to make them is in the appendix.

# JULY

Jul 1 – Jul 24 Tour de France

Jul 3 – Aug 11 Dog Days

Jul 3 – Aug 15 Air Conditioning Appreciation Days

Jul 23 – 26 World Maccabiah Games

Jul 29 — Aug 3 Transplant Games of America

## Month-Long Holidays

Cell Phone Courtesy Month • Fireworks Safety Month • International Alopecia Month for Women • National Deli Salad Month • National "Doghouse Repairs" Month • National Grilling Month • National Horseradish Month • National Hot Dog Month • National Ice Cream Month • National Make a Difference to Children Month • National Minority Mental Health Awareness Month • National Park and Recreation Month • National Watermelon Month • Sarcoma Awareness Month • Smart Irrigation Month • Women's Motorcycle Month • Worldwide Bereaved Parents Awareness Month

## Week-Long Holidays

Jul 1 – 7 National Independent Living Week

Jul 3 – 9 Be Nice to Jersey Week • National Farrier's Week

Jul 4 – 10 National Marijuana Facts Week • Nude Recreation Week

Jul 10 – 17 Sports Cliché Week

Jul 11 – 17 Scotland: The Open

Jul 17 – 23 Captive Nations Week

Jul 21 – 23 Sloppy Joe's Hemingway® Look-alike Contest

Jul 21 – 24 Comic–Con International

Jul 23 – 31 National Moth Week

Jul 24 – 30 Women in Baseball Week

Jul 30 – Aug 6 England Cowes Week

Jul 31 – Aug 1 Moby Dick Marathon

Jul 31 – Aug 6 National Exercise with Your Child Week

Jul 23 – 25 Japan: Soma No Umaoi (Wild Horse Chasing)

# Daily Holidays

1. Botswana: Sir Seretse Khama Day • Burundi: Independence Day • Canada: Canada Day • China: Half-year Day • *First Photographs Used in Newspaper Report (1848) • *First Scheduled Television Broadcast (1941) • Ghana: Republic Day • India: Ratha Yatra • Medicare Day • Postage Stamp Day • Resolution Renewal Day • Rwanda: Independence Day • Somalia Democratic Republic: National Day • Suriname: Liberation Day • *Zip Code Day • Zoo Day

2. Amelia Earhart Disappears (1937) • *Civil Rights Day • *Constitution Day (USA) • Declaration of Independence Resolution (1776) • First Solo Round-the-World Balloon Flight (2002) • Halfway Point Day • United Nations: International Day of Cooperative

3. Air-conditioning Appreciation Days • Belarus: Independence Day • *Compliment Your Mirror Day • Independence Sunday in Iowa • Quebec Founded (1608) • *Stay Out of the Sun Day

4. *America the Beautiful Day • Caribbean Day or Caricom Day • Declaration of Independence Signing (1776) • Earth at Aphelion Day • *Fourth of July or Independence Day • *Anne Landers (1918) • *Lou Gehrig Day (1939) • Philippines: Fil American Friendship Day • Zambia: Heroes Day

5. Algeria: Independence Day • *Bikini Day • Cape Verde: National Day • First Cloning of an Animal Day (1996) • Isle of Man: Tynwald Day • *National Labor Relations Day • Slovakia: Saint Cyril and Methodius Day • Venezuela: Independence Day • Zambia: Unity Day

6. Comoros: Independence Day • Czech Republic: Commemoration Day of Burning of John Hus • First Airship Crossing of the Atlantic (1919) • First Successful Anti-rabies Inoculation (1885) • Lithuania: Day of Statehood • Luxembourg: Ettelbruck Remembrance Day • Malawi: Republic Day • Republican Party Day • *Take Your Webmaster to Lunch Day

7. *Bonza Bottler Day™ • *Father–Daughter Take a Walk Together Day • Solomon Islands: Independence Day • Spain: Running of the Bulls • Tanzania: Saba Saba Day

8. Aspinwall Crosses US on Horseback (1911) • National Motorcycle Day • *SCUD Day (Savor the Comic, Unplug the Drama)

9. Argentina: Independence Day • Bald is In Day • Carver Day • First Open-Heart Surgery Day (1893) • Highest Tsunami in Recorded History Day (1958) • Morocco: Youth Day • South Sudan: Independence Day

10. Bahamas: Independence Day • *Clerihew Day • *Don't Step on a Bee Day • Martyrdom of the Bab • Stone House Day

11. Bowdler's Day • *Day of the Five Billion • International Town Criers Day • Make Your Own Sundae Day • Mongolia: Naadam National Holiday • *United Nations: World Population Day

12. Different Colored Eyes Day • Family Feud Day (1976) • Kiribati: Independence Day • National Pecan Pie Day • Northern Ireland: Orangemen's Day • Sao Tome and Principe: Independence Day

13. *Embrace Your Geekness Day • France: Night Watch (La Retraite Aux Flambeaux • *Gruntled Workers Day • "Live Aid" Day • National Beef Tallow Day • National French Fry Day • National Nitrogen Ice Cream Day • Republic of Montenegro: National Day • World Cup Day (1930)

14. England: Birmingham Riots Day (1791) • France: Night Watch (Bastille Day)

15. Japan: Bon (Feast of Lanterns) • *Rembrandt Day • Saint Swithin's Day • United Nations: World Youth Skills Day

16. Amazon Incorporated (1995) • Atomic Bomb Test Day (1945) • Boliva: La Paz Day • Get to Know Your Customers Day (third Thursday of each quarter is set aside to get to know your customers even better) • National Bride Sale Day • National Woodie Wagon Day • Toss Away the "Could Haves" and "Should Haves" Day • Women's Dive Day

17. Astor Day • Disneyland Opened (1955) • Korea: Constitution Day • Minimum Legal Drinking Age at 21 • National Ice Cream Day • Puerto Rico: Muñoz–Rivera Day • World Emoji Day • "Wrong Way" Corrigan Day (1938)

18. Japan: Marine Day • Mandela Day • National Get Out of the Doghouse Day • Tisha B'av or Fast of Ab • Uruguay: Constitution Day

19. Elvis Presley First Single Day • Nicaragua: National Liberation Day • Saint Vincent de Paul Day

20. Columbia: Independence Day • Geneva Accords (1954) • International Balloon Dog Day • Riot Act Day • *Special Olympics Day • Take Your Poet to Work Day • United Nations: World Chess Day

21. Belgium: Independence Day • Get to Know Your Customers Day (third Thursday of each quarter is set aside to get to know your customers even better) • Guam: Liberation Day • *Hemingway Day (1899) • Lowest Recorded Temperature Day (1983) • No Pet Store Puppies Day

22. *Pied Piper Day • *Rat–catchers Day • *Spooner's (Spoonerism) Day

23. Egypt: Revolution Day • *Hot Enough for Ya Day • National Day of the Cowboy

24. Auntie's Day® • *Cousins Day • Amelia Earhart Day • *National Drive-Thru Day • Pioneer Day

25. Costa Rica: Guanacast Day • First Airplane Crossing of English Channel (1909) • Puerto Rico: Constitution Day • Spain: Saint James Day • Tunisia: Republic Day

26. Americans with Disabilities Day • Armed Forces Unified (1947) • Cuba: National Day (1953) • Curaçao Day • International Day for the Conservation of the Mangrove Ecosystem • Liberia and Maldives: Independence Day • Potsdam Declaration (1945) • *George Bernard Shaw (1856) • *US Army Desegregation Day (1944)

27. *Atlantic Telegraph Day • *National Korean War Veterans Armistice Day • *Take Your Houseplant for a Walk Day • *Walk on Stilts Day

28. Peru: Independence Day • Beatrix Potter Day • Thailand: King's Birthday and National Day • World Hepatitis Day • World War I Begins (1914)

29. Global Tiger Day • Lord of the Rings Day • *NASA (1958) • Norway: Olsok Eve • Rain Day • Spain: Festival of Near-Death Experiences

30. Insulin First Isolated and Extracted Day (1921) • Islamic New Year • National Cheesecake Day • *Paperback Books (1935) • United Nations: International Day of Friendship • United Nations: World Day Against Trafficking in Persons • Vanuatu: Independence Day

31. National Mutt Day • *US Patent Office Opened (1790) • World Ranger Day

# Holiday Marketing Ideas

**Jul 31 – Aug 1 Moby Dick Marathon** — Are you a fan of the classics? This tale is one of those that spans generations. To promote your business, you could host a read-a-thon. Bring your best storytelling skills and invite other readers to join you. Throughout the 24-hours of the holiday take turns reading sections or chapters and see just how much of the book you can read. Have some fun while you are at it and share puzzles and games. Here's how it would work to your benefit.

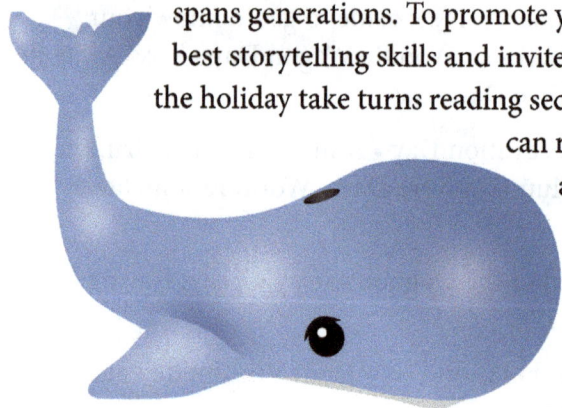

Each speaker hides a whale on their website. Then once they have read their chapter or section, the attendees have to go to the speaker's website and find their hidden whale. At the end of the event, the person with the most whales in their possession wins a prize.

Not only does it get your attendees familiar with your speaker's offerings, but it will increase your SEO at the same time!

To make it even easier for you, I've created a small whale graphic that you are welcome to use. You'll find it located in the appendix.

**Jul 3 Stay Out of the Sun Day** — This is a day to increase awareness of skin cancer. Infographics, tips, and social media are a good place to start. However, if you want to garner media attention for your business, you might consider hosting or sponsoring a drive to raise funds to donate to help fund cancer research. If you can get a large company to offer a matching funds when you reach a certain level of contributions, then you have yourself a win-win-win all around.

**Jul 11 United Nations: World Population Day** — The theme of today is 'diversity'. Since it is a United Nations official holiday why not go huge? Contact your local business community through your Chamber of Commerce and put together a Folk Festival. Here in America, we have American Indians, Greeks, Italians, Swiss, Germans, Indians, and many others who have special dances, clothes, and traditions that would be more than happy to participate in an event that would showcase their heritage.

Become a sponsor or even just a vendor at the event and notify the media to help promote and cover it.

If you are looking to do something a bit less over-the-top, social media graphics or even blog or radio tours might be of interest to you. Share facts about your heritage or promote a book or product produced by your ancestors. It might just be as simple as having a recipe swap of various ethnic cuisines.

**Jul 29 Global Tiger Day** — Grrrreat things are in store for your business when you sink your teeth into this marketing opportunity. Think about ways to get the word out about your products and services while putting your purrfectly planned sales strategy into action.

Of course, social media is always an easy choice. Nevertheless, you have to agree that tigers are not just cute little pussy cats. So, it's up to you to push beyond those simple ideas and chase after a bigger solution.

One sure way to do that is to pounce on the inspiration that event planning can provide. With tigers being the theme of the day, I suggest you look for speakers who can help others in big ways. Topic could include such things as taking charge of their finances, learning how to write marketing copy, communication skills, dress for success, public speaking, and many others.

# AUGUST

Aug 5 – 14 Sturgis Rally
Aug 12 – Sep 4 Spain: Vuelta a España
Aug 29 – Sep 11 US Open Tennis Championship

## Month-Long Holidays

American Adventures Month • Black Business Month • Boomers Making a Difference Month • Children's Eye Health and Safety Month • Children's Vision and Learning Month • International EFT Tapping Month • International Pirate Month • National Immunization Awareness Month • National Minority Donor Awareness Month • National Spinal Muscular Atrophy Awareness Month • Read-a-Romance Month • What Will Be Your Legacy Month

## Week-Long Holidays

Aug 1 – 5 Psychic Week
Aug 1 – 7 International Clown Week (first full week) • National Bargain Hunting Week • World Breastfeeding Week
Aug 7 – 13 Assistance Dog Week
Aug 9 – 13 Perseid Meteor Showers
Aug 9 – 17 Elvis Week
Aug 14 – 20 National Aviation Week
Aug 25 – 31 Be Kind to Humankind Week
Aug 25 – 28 Hotter 'n Hell Hundred Bike Race
Aug 27 – 28 Belgium: Wedding of the Giants

## Daily Holidays

1. Australia: Picnic Day • Bahamas: Emancipation Day • Benin: Independence Day • Canada: Civic Holiday, Colorado Day • Emancipation of 500 Day • *Girlfriend's Day • Grenada: Emancipation Day • Iceland and Ireland: August Holiday, Jamaica and Niger: Independence Day • *Lughnasadh • Rounds Resounding Day • *Spiderman Day • Switzerland: Confederation Day • Trinidad and Tobago: Emancipation Day • United Kingdom: Minden Day • *US Census Day (1790) • *US Customs Day • World Lung Cancer Day • *World Wide Web or Internaut Day (2017) • Zambia: Youth Day

2. Costa Rica: Feast of Our Lady of Angels • *Declaration of Independence: Official Signing (1776) • Macedonia: National Day • National Night Out Day

3. Columbus Sails for the New World (1492) • Equatorial Guinea: Armed Forces Day • Guinea-Bissau: Colonization Martyrs' Day • National Watermelon Day • Niger: Independence Day

4. *Louis Armstrong Day • Burkina Faso: Revolution Day • Croatia: Homeland Thanksgiving Day • Queen Elizabeth Day

5. Braham Pie Day • Burkina Faso: Republic Day • First English Colony in North America (1583)

6. Atomic Bomb Dropped on Hiroshima (1945) • Bolivia: Independence Day • Death Penalty Day • Fancy Farm Picnic Day,*Hiroshima Day • *Jamaica: Independence Achieved (1962) • National Mustard Day • Voting Rights Day (1965)

7. Columbia: Battle of Boyaca Day • Cote D'Ivoire: National Day • Hatfield-McCoy Feud Eruption Day • Herbert Hoover Day (Sunday nearest Aug 10th) • *Mata Hari Day (1876) • National Lighthouse Day • *Particularly Preposterous Packaging Day • *Professional Speakers Day • Sister's Day® • Tisha B'Av or Fast of AB • US War Department Day • World Trade Center Tightrope Walk Day

8. Ashura: Tenth Day • *Bonza Bottler Day™ • Digital Nomad Day • Happiness Happens Day • National Fried Chicken and Waffles Day • *Sneak Some Zucchini onto Your Neighbor's Porch Night • Tanzania: Farmers' Day • Victory Day • Wear Your Mother's Jewelry Day

9. Atomic Bomb Dropped on Nagasaki (1945) • Bahamas: Fox Hill Day (second Tuesday in August) • Japan: Moment of Silence (Bombing of Nagasaki) • *Moment of Silence Day • Singapore: National Day • South Africa: National Women's Day • *United Nations: International Day of The World's Indigenous Peoples • *Veep Day

10. *Candid Camera Day • Ecuador Independence Day • National S'mores Day • Nestlé Day (1814) • *Smithsonian Day • World Lion Day

11. Chadd: Independence Day • *Alex Haley Day (1921) • Japan: Yama No Hi (Mountain Day) • Saint Clare of Assisi: Feast Day • Zimbabwe: Heroes' Day

12. *Home Sewing Machine Day • *IBM PC Day • Night of the Murdered Poets • Thailand: Birthday of the Queen • *United Nations: International Youth Day • *Vinyl Record Day

13. Berlin Wall Erected (1961) • Central African Republic: Independence Day • *Alfred Hitchcock (1899) • *International Left Hander's Day • Middle Children's Day • National Garage Sale Day,*Annie Oakley Day (1860) • Lucy Stone Day (1818),Tunisia: Women's Day

14. *Navajo Nation: Code Talkers Day • Pakistan: Independence Day • *Social Security Day • V–J Day (1945)

15. *Assumption of the Virgin Mary • *Best Friends Day • Canada: Yukon Discovery Day • *Chauvin Day • Check the Chip Day • Congo (Brazzaville): National Day • Equatorial Guinea: Constitution Day • Green Data Day • Hirohito's Radio Address (1945) • India and Korea: Independence Day • Liechtenstein: National Day • *National Relaxation Day • *Panama Canal Day (1914) • Transcontinental US Railway Completion (1870) • *Woodstock (1969)

16. Dominican Republic: Restoration of the Republic • National Roller Coaster Day • Surveillance Day

17. Balloon Crossing of Atlantic Ocean (1978) • Black Cat Appreciation Day • *Clinton's "Meaning of 'Is'" Day (1998) • *Davy Crockett (1786) • Gabon and Indonesia: Independence Day • *Mae West Day (1893)

18. *Bad Poetry Day • *Birth Control Pills Day • *Mail–Order Catalog Day • Serendipity Day

19. Afghanistan: Independence Day • Don Ho Day (1930) • India: Krishna Janmashtami • United Nations: World Humanitarian Day

20. Hungary: Saint Stephen's Day • International Geocaching Day • International Homeless Animals Day® and Candlelight Vigils • Morocco: Revolution of the King and the People • *Plutonium Day

21. Alexandria Library Sit-in Day • *American Bar Association Day • *Poet's Day • Seminole Tribe Day (1953) • United Nations: International Day of Remembrance and Tribute to the Victims of Terrorism

22. *Be an Angel Day • *International Yacht Race Day • Mormon Choir Day • *Southern Hemisphere Hoodie-Hoo Day • Vietnam Conflict Begins (1945)

23. First Man-Powered Flight (1977) • *United Nations: Day for the Remembrance of the slave trade and its abolition • *Valentino Day

24. Liberia: Flag Day • *Pluto Demoted Day • Ukraine: Independence Day • *Vesuvius Day • William Wilberforce Day

25. Founders Day • *Kiss-and-Make-Up Day • *National Park Service Day • Uruguay: Independence Day • *Wizard of Oz Day (1939)

26. Baseball Day (First Televised, 1939) • Namibia and Philippines: Heroes' Day • *National Dog Day • *Women's Equality Day

27. International Bat Night • Moldova: Independence Day • *Mother Teresa Day • *"The Duchess" Who Wasn't Day

28. *March on Washington (1963) • National Weed Out Hate Day • *Race Your Mouse Around the Icons Day • *Radio Commercials Day

29. *According to Hoyle Day • Hong Kong: Liberation Day • *More Herbs, Less Salt Day • Philippines: National Heroes' Day • Slovakia: National Uprising Day • United Nations: International Day Against Nuclear Tests

30. Huey P Long Day • Peru: Saint Rose of Lima Day • Turkey: Victory Day • United Nations: International Day of Victims of Enforced Disappearances

31. International Overdose Awareness Day • Kazakhstan and Kyrgyzstan: Constitution Day and Independence Day • Klondike Eldorado Gold Discovery Day • *Love Litigating Lawyers Day • Malaysia: Freedom Day • Moldova: National Language Day • Spain: La Tomatina (Tomato Food Fight Festival) • Trinidad and Tobago: Independence Day

# Holiday Marketing Ideas

**What Will Be Your Legacy Month** — Did you realize there is a holiday for this? As you contemplate the answer to this question consider how you can help others define their goals. The topics for today could range from goal setting to estate planning. I think you'll agree that is a wide range.

Since you have the entire month to celebrate this holiday, you could host a daily topic and either post tips or host a daily speaker.

If you are into podcasting or blogging, you have the perfect venue to host your month-long event.

**Aug 1 Spiderman Day** — It's time to check your spider senses. A favorite superhero, Spiderman is best known for his witty one-liners and down-to-earth personality. So today, ramp up your wit and share a few one-liners of your own. Share them on social media in graphics that showcase this superhero. If you can't think of any one-liners, then you could always share a factoid or two. You'll find a few in the appendix that you are welcome to use either as text only or in your own social media graphics.

**Aug 6 Fancy Farm Picnic Day** — This holiday is celebrated in Kentucky in a big way! With the focus on bar-b-que and political speeches dominating the day. However, your celebration could follow a different one of their concepts. It is held to raise funds for a specific charity. So, why not choose a local charity and attempt to raise funds for them.

Fund raising will require a bit of work, but with the right team behind you, it can be a worthwhile endeavor. Be sure to let your media know what you are up to for the best results and a bit of press showcasing your business, your event, and your event sponsors.

For instruction on how to raise funds for your favorite charity look in the appendix where I have pulled the information from GoFundMe.com to help you get started.

**Aug 8 Wear Your Mother's Jewelry Day** — Do you sell jewelry? If so, you have the perfect holiday for your business. If not, why not consider how wearing all that bling makes you feel? Or how about a Dress for Success presentation? You could teach others how to dress to represent their brands or while giving a presentation. This could segue into proper grooming, make-up application, and even how to sit properly when on stage.

Then there's always jewelry making classes. How fun would that be? You wouldn't even have to hold it in person. When you make it an online event you could end up having folks join you from all across the globe. Or, instead of creating an event, why not share a video on any of the above-mentioned subjects? Videos are the hot marketing tools these days, so why not take advantage of them?

**Aug 13 Lucy Stone Day** — Women worldwide should take special note of this holiday. You don't know who she is? What is she famous for doing? The answer is that Lucy Stone, back in 1847, became the first woman from Massachusetts to earn a college degree. She spoke out for women's rights and against slavery. Lucy was a prominent U.S. orator, abolitionist, and suffragist, and a vocal advocate and organizer promoting rights for women.

Now that you know who she was does that give you any ideas? Do I hear a rallying cry for the under privileged in our society? In honor of Lucy Stone Day any activity that helps the less fortunate in your area could be good for body and soul.

Volunteer at a local school or even a nursing home. Help put together a clothing or food drive? Share some words of wisdom with the younger generation. All of these ideas and more are terrific ways to spend your day.

**Aug 18 Mail Order Catalog Day**—It's time to support your online friends' storefronts. The order of the day is a super spectacular buying event. Invite everyone you know to join you in a pre-Christmas extravaganza. Each seller should be given a bit of time to introduce their offering. If you put together a 'links' page where all the sellers are listed be sure to include at least one 'testimonial review' per seller.

As I mentioned regarding a previous holiday, you might even want to include a hidden symbol, perhaps an envelope, on each seller's website and the buyer who collects the most wins a prize. Be sure to make it a valuable prize to make it worth their time.

**Aug Day 28 Radio Commercials Day**—Podcasts and radio are great tools to get your message out to the masses. So, today perhaps you could help others by sharing tips, graphics, infographics, or even a webinar to help them along the way. How to present on air, how to write ad copy, and how to design an ad are all great ideas that would be greatly appreciated by your audience. Oh, and don't forget to at least put one ad on air yourself.

# SEPTEMBER

Sep 10–25 XIX ASAID 2022 Asian Games
Sep 15–Oct 15 National Hispanic Heritage Month
Sep 17–Oct 12 Germany: Octoberfest

## Month-Long Holidays

Atrial Fibrillation Awareness Month • Be Kind to Editors and Writers Month • Childhood Cancer Awareness Month • Chili: National Month • Fall Hat Month • Gynecologic Cancer Awareness Month • Happy Cat Month • Hunger Action Month • Library Card Sign-Up Month • Mold Awareness Month • National Cholesterol Education Month • National Head Lice Prevention Month • National Honey Month • National Mushroom Month • National Preparedness Month • National Prostate Cancer Awareness Month • National Recovery Month • National Rice Month • National Service Dog Month • One-on-One Month • Ovarian Cancer Awareness Month • Pleasure Your Mate Month • September Is Healthy Aging® Month • Sports Eye Safety Month • Subliminal Communications Month • Update Your Resume Month • Worldwide Speak Out Month • Youth Leadership Month

## Week-Long Holidays

Sep 1–4 England: Land Rover Burghley Horse Trials
Sep 1–7 Brazil: Independence Week
Sep 1–10 Substitute Teacher Appreciation Week
Sep 5–9 National Payroll Week
Sep 11–17 Be a Mensch Week • National Security Officer Appreciation Week • United Kingdom: Battle of Britain Week
Sep 12–17 National Line Dance Week
Sep 17–23 Constitution Week
Sep 18–24 Build a Better Image Week • International Go-Kart Week • National Farm Safety and Health Week • National Singles Week • Tolkien Week • World Reflexology Week
Sep 19–25 International Week of the Deaf
Sep 25–Oct 1 Banned Books Week—Celebrating the Freedom to Read
Sep 26–27 Rosh Hashanah Jewish New Year

# Daily Holidays

1. 1. Benton Neighbor Day • *Edgar Rice Burroughs (1875) • Chicken Boy's Birthday,*Emma M. Nutt Day • Japan: Kanto Earthquake Memorial Day • National Toy Testing Day • Orthodox Ecclesiastical New Year • Slovakia: Constitution Day • Titanic Discovery Day • Uzbekistan: Independence Day • WWII Begins (1939)

2. Bring Your Manners to Work Day • Calendar Adjustment Day • US Treasury Department Founded Day • Vietnam: Independence Day • *V–J Day

3. Penny Press Day (1833) • Qatar: Independence Day • San Marino: National Day

4. Curaçao: Animal's Day • Electric Lights Day • *Newspaper Carrier Day

5. Canada and US: Labor Day (first Monday in September) • First Continental Congress Assembly (1774) • First Labor Day Observance (1882) • Jesse James Day (1847) • Michigan's Great Fire of 1881 • United Nations: International Day of Charity

6. Jane Addams Day • Baltic States: Independence Day • Bulgaria: Unification Day • Pakistan: Defense of Pakistan Day • Swaziland: Independence Day

7. Brazil: Independence Day • *Google Commemoration Day (1998) • *Grandma Moses Day • *Neither Snow nor Rain Day Day • Queen Elizabeth I Birthday (1533) • United Nations: International Day of Clean Air for Blue Skies Day

8. Andorra: National Holiday • Huey P. Long Shot Day • Macedonia: Independence Day • Malta: Victory Day • Pediatric Hematology/Oncology Nurses Day • Star Trek Day • Tarzan Day • *United Nations: International Literacy Day

9. *Bonza Bottler Day™ • Japan: Chrysanthemum Day • Korea • Democratic People's Republic of: National Day • Luxembourg: Liberation Ceremony • National Day of Prayer and Remembrance • National Dog Walker Appreciation Day • Tajikistan: Independence Day • United Nations: International Day to Protect Education from Attack • *Wonderful Weirdos Day

10. Belize: Saint George's Caye Day • China: Teacher's Day • Prairie Day • Swap Ideas Day • World Suicide Prevention Day

11. *Attack on America Day • Catalonia: National Day of Catalonia • Ethiopia: New Year's Day • *Food Stamps Day • National Grandparents' Day • *Patriot Day and National Day of Service and Remembrance

12. Defenders Day • Guinea-Bissau: National Holiday • National Boss/Employee Exchange Day • United Nations: Day for South-South Cooperation • Video Games Day

13. 9 x 13 Day • Kids Take Over the Kitchen Day • *National Celiac Awareness Day • Roald Dahl Day • United Nations: Opening Day of General Assembly

14. Gravitational Waves First Detected (2015) • Nicaragua: Battle of San Jacinto Day • *Solo Transatlantic Balloon Crossing (1984)

15. *Agatha Christie Day • Costa Rica and El Salvador: Independence Day • *First National Convention for Blacks (1830) • Greenpeace Founded (1971) • Guatemala, Honduras, and Nicaragua: Independence Day • Quarterly Estimated Federal Income Tax Payers' Due Date (also

Jan 17, Apr 15, and June 15, 2022) • United Kingdom: Battle of Britain Day • *United Nations: International Day of Democracy

16. *Anne Dudley Bradstreet Day • Cherokee Strip Day • General Motors Day • *Great Seal of the US (1782) • Malaysia: Malaysia Day (Hari Malaysia) • Mayflower Day (1620) • Mexico: Independence Day • National POW/MIA Recognition (the third Friday in September) • Papua New Guinea: Independence Day • *United Nations: International Day for the Preservation of the Ozone Layer • World Play-Doh Day

17. Angola: Day of the National Hero • Batman Day • *Citizenship Day • *Constitution Day (1787) • International Coastal Cleanup • International Red Panda Day • Locate an Old Friend Day • National Constitution Center Constitution Day • National Football League Formed Day (1920) • National Table Shuffleboard Day • VFW Ladies Auxiliary Day • World Patient Safety Day

18. Chile: Independence Day • Get Smart Day • National Cheeseburger Day • National HIV/AIDS and Aging Awareness Day • *US Air Force Birthday • *US Capitol Cornerstone Laid • US Takes Out its First Loan (1789)

19. *"Iceman" Mummy Discovered (1991) • *International Talk Like a Pirate Day • Japan: Respect for the Aged Day • Saint Christopher (Saint Kitts) and Nevis: Independence Day

20. *Billie Jean King Wins Battle of the Sexes (1973) • Financial Panic Day • Fonzie Jumps the Shark Day • International Day of University Sport • IT Professionals Day • *National Equal Rights Founded (1884) • Netherlands: Prinsjesdag

21. Armenia, Belize, and Malta: Independence Day • National School Backpack Awareness Day • National Surgical Technologists Day • *United Nations: International Day of Peace

22. American Business Woman's Day • Dear Diary Day • *Emancipation Proclamation (1862) • Hobbit Day • Ice Cream Cone Day • Long Count Day (1927) • Mabon (Alban Elfed) • Mali: Independence Day • National Centenarian's Day • National Walk 'n' Roll Dog Day • Remember Me Thursday® • Remote Employee Appreciation Day • US Postmaster General's Day (1789)

23. Baseball's Greatest Dispute Day • *Celebrate Bisexuality Day • Checkers Day • Innergize Day • Japan: Autumnal Equinox Day • *Lewis and Clark Expedition Returns (1806) • Planet Neptune Discovery (1846) • Saudi Arabia: Kingdom Unification • United Nations: International Day of Sign Languages

24. Cambodia: Constitutional Declaration Day • Daniel Boone Day • Fish Amnesty Day • Guinea-Bissau: Independence Day • Mozambique: Armed Forces Day • National Public Lands Day • *National Punctuation Day • Schwenkfelder Thanksgiving • South Africa: Heritage Day

25. Acne Scar Awareness Day • *First American Newspaper Published (1690) • Gold Star Mother's and Family Day (always the last Sunday in September) • *Greenwich Mean Time Begins (1676) • International Day of the Deaf • National One Hit Wonder Day • National Psychotherapy Day • Pacific Ocean Discovered (1513) • Rosh Hashanah (begins at sundown) • Rwanda: Republic Day

26. *Johnny Appleseed Day • United Nations: International Day for the Total Elimination of Nuclear Weapons

27. *Samuel Adams (1722) • *Ancestor Appreciation Day • Ethiopia: True Cross Day • Rabi'l: The Month of Migration • Saint Vincent de Paul Feast Day • *World Tourism Day

28. Banned Websites Awareness Day • *Cabrillo Day • Taiwan: Confucius and Teachers' Day • United Nations/UNESCO: International Day for Universal Access to Information • World Rabies Day

29. Michelangelo Antonio (1912) • Michaelmas • National Biscotti Day • National Coffee Day • Paraguay: Boquerón Day • Scotland Yard Day (1829) • Silent Movie Day • United Nations: International Day of Awareness of Food Loss and Waste Reduction • United Nations: World Maritime Day • Veterans of Foreign Wars Day

30. Botswana: Independence Day • First Criminal Execution in America Day (1630) • Gutenberg Bible Published (1452) • Hug a Vegan Day • International Translation Day • Saint Jerome: Feast Day

# Holiday Marketing Ideas

**Youth Leadership Month** —This month we look to those who are younger than we are. That doesn't mean they have to be teens, but if they are, that's what this holiday is about. Tips and quotes are always a good idea for social media exposer. Don't forget to brand them to your business for the marketing to show your support.

As you might expect, events are the key to any well thought out marketing plan. If you sponsor or host an event, that will give you even more exposure than just participating in one.

Gather a group of trainers, maybe even a career coach or two. You could also consider asking a fashion and makeup consultant to participate in your event. And, if you hold a large enough event be sure to let the media know what you are up to for maximum exposure. I'm thinking an Expo!

**Sep 2 Bring Your Manners to Work Day** —It's time to put your cell phone on mute and get some work done. Manners are not outdated. However, both young and seasoned folks, don't know what proper etiquette entails. Perhaps you could share from your experience. Social media posting is a good start, but if you are a coach or consultant, you might do well to schedule a podcast or radio show appearance. My advice is to start local and work your way up from there. Don't just go for the "big time" until you have proven yourself capable of being an effective talk show guest.

**Sep 8 Tarzan Day** —It's time to swing into action! To promote your business with a nod toward Tarzan we simply have to develop a theme that encompasses attributes of Tarzan. To that end, I'll help you by giving you the first thoughts that enter my periphery. Tarzan was: a lover of nature (street or beach cleanup) • seeker of justice (legal advice) • lived in the jungle treetops (reach new highs in your business) • lost at birth

and raised by apes (adoption) • adventurer (grow your business by mastering serious challenges) • and limited language skills (communication skills).

Now, if that list doesn't inspire you to devise a way to promote your business with Tarzan Day as your theme, you'll just have to don your thinking cap.

**Sep 10 Swap Ideas Day**—Here's a business building holiday for you. Things like starting a mentoring or mastermind group are excellent ideas of how to spend this weird & wacky holiday. Since this is Youth Leadership Month • consider speaking at a local educational establishment.

If you have people who work with or for you, why not have them join you to share their thoughts on how you can improve your business. If they are subcontractors, be sure to include offer to help them improve their bottom line as well as yours. Sounds like a win-win to me!

**Sep 16 World Play-Doh Day**—Today is all about having a bit of fun. Did you know you can make your own 'playdough' at home? I have included the directions for both a cooked and uncooked version in the Samples Appendix that you can use and share.

What about playdough creations? Invite others to share their creations online. Create a Pinterest page to showcase all their submitted handiwork. Be sure to use the hashtag #Play-Doh and #Playdough on social media to see how others are celebrating this weird & wacky holiday.

**Sep 17 Locate an Old Friend Day**—My first thought when I saw this weird & wacky holiday was that contacting your customers and clients in a kind and friendly way could be a wise investment of your time. Simply send them a note or card through snail mail (I've explained why snail mail is better than email in previous editions.) to thank them for their loyalty. While you are at it you might mention a new product or service you provide that they might not be aware of. A good example from my own business is that I recently began offering screenplay formatting. Do you have a similar offer to inform them of? Now, is the perfect time to do so.

If you aren't afraid to pick up the phone, you might even want to call them just to wish them a happy holiday.

**Sep 22 Remote Employee Appreciation**—With the pandemic continuing to keep many of us working from home this is an appropriate weird & wacky holiday to add to your marketing mix.

If you have clients or customers who you know are working remotely let them know you are available to support them and help them grow their business (yours could benefit too).

A social media graphic is also a way to brand your business while using this weird & wacky holiday to let them know you are thinking about them. You'll find one I created for you that you can brand and share in the appendix.

# OCTOBER

Oct 7 Rabi'i: The Month of Migration (begins)
Oct 24 – Nov 11 World Origami Days

## Month-Long Holidays

Adopt-A-Shelter-Dog Month • Antidepressant Death Awareness Month • Bat Appreciation Month • Breast Cancer Awareness Month • Celebrating the Bilingual Child Month • Contact Lens Safety Month • Domestic Violence Awareness Month • Dyslexia Awareness Month • Emotional Intelligence Awareness Month • Gay and Lesbian History Month • German American Heritage Month • Global Diversity Awareness Month • Go Hog Wild—Eat Country Ham Month • Health Literacy Month • Inktober • National Audiology Awareness Month • National Breast Cancer Awareness Month • National Bullying Prevention Awareness Month • National Chiropractic Health Month • National Crime Prevention Month • National Critical Illness Awareness Month • National Cybersecurity Awareness Month • National Dental Hygiene Month • National Disability Employment Awareness Month • National Domestic Violence Awareness Month • National Down Syndrome Awareness Month • National Medical Librarians Month • National Orthodontic Health Month • National Physical Therapy Month • National Polish American Heritage Month • National Popcorn Poppin' Month • National Reading Group Month • National Roller Skating Month • National Seafood Month • National Spina Bifida Awareness Month • National Stamp Collecting Month • National Stop Bullying Month • National Work and Family Month • Organize Your Medical Information Month • Positive Attitude Month • Rett Syndrome Awareness Month • Squirrel Awareness and Appreciation Month • Teentober • Vegetarian Awareness Month • Workplace Politics Awareness Month • World Menopause Month

## Week-Long Holidays

Oct 3 – 9 Mental Illness Awareness Week • National Carry a Tune Week

Oct 4 – 10 United Nations: World Space Week

Oct 9 – 15 Earth Science Week • Fire Prevention Week • National Metric Week • Take Your Medicine Americans Week

Oct 10 – 14 National School Lunch Week

Oct 15 – 20 Japan: Newspaper Week

Oct 16 – 22 Bullying Bystanders Unite Week • National Character Counts Week • National Chemistry Week • National Food Bank Week • National Forest Products Week • National Friends of Libraries Week • Rodent Awareness Week

Oct 17 – 21 Nuclear Science Week

Oct 19 – 23 Germany: Frankfurt Book Fair

Oct 23 – 29 Prescription Errors Education and Awareness Week

Oct 24 – 30 United Nations: Disarmament Week

Oct 25 – 31 International Magic Week

# Daily Holidays

1. 1. Bed and Breakfast Inn Mascot Day • China: National Day • Cyberspace Day • Cyprus: Independence Day • Fall Astronomy Day • *Fire Pup Day • Kids Music Day • International Beautiful World Day • Model-T Day • Nigeria: Independence Day • Night of the Living Dead Day • South Korea: Armed Forces Day • This is Your Life Day • Tuvalu: Independence Day • United Nations: International Day of Older Persons • US 2022 Federal Fiscal Year Begins • World Vegetarian Day

2. Blessing of the Fishing Fleet Gandhi Day • Country Inn, Bed-and-Breakfast Day • *Guardian Angels Day • Guinea: Independence Day • *Groucho Marx (1890) • *National Custodial Workers Day • National G.E.O. (Growth.Overcome.Empower) Day,*"Peanuts" Debut Day (1950) • United Nations: International Day of Nonviolence • World Communion Sunday • World Day for Farmed Animals

3. Child Health Day (first Monday in October) • Germany: Day of German Unity • Honduras: Francisco Morazán Holiday • Korea: Tangun Day (National Foundation Day) • *Mickey Mouse Club Day (1955) • Netherlands: Relief of Leiden Day • United Nations: World Habitat Day • World Day of Bullying Prevention™

4. *Dick Tracy Day (1931) • *Gregorian Calendar Adjustment Day • International Ships-In-Bottles Day • Lesotho: Independence Day • National Taco Day • *Ten-Four Day • World Child Development Day • Yom Kippur (begins at sundown)

5. Duputren Disease Awareness Day • India: Dasara (Dissehra) • International Walk to School Day • Portugal: Republic Day • Random Acts of Poetry Day,*United Nations: World Teachers Day • Yom Kippur

6. *American Library Association Day • Egypt: Armed Forces Day • Ireland: Ivy Day • *Jackie Mayer Rehab Day • National Depression Screening Day • *National German American Day • National Noodle Day • United Kingdom: National Badger Day • United Kingdom: National Poetry Day

7. Kids Music Day • National Diversity Day • World Smile Day

8. Croatia: Statehood Day • *Great Chicago Fire (1871) • International Migratory Bird Day • National Hydrogen and Fuel Cell Day • National Pierogy Day • National Salmon Day • Peshtigo Forest Fire (1871) • Universal Music Day • *Alvin C. York Day

9. Father-Daughter Day • Grandmother's Day in Florida • Groundhog Day • Korea: Hangul (Alphabet Day) • *Leif Erickson Day • National Nanotechnology Day • Peru: Day of National Honor • Samoa and American Samoa: White Sunday • Sukkot (begins at sundown) • Uganda: Independence Day • *United Nations: World Post Day

10. *Bonza Bottler Day™ • Canada: Thanksgiving Day • Columbus Day • Discoverer's Day in Hawaii • *Double 10 Day • Fiji: Independence Day • Indigenous Peoples Day • Japan: Sports Day • National Handbag Day • National Kick Butt Day • Native Americans' Day (South Dakota) • Oklahoma Historical Day • Sukkot • *Tuxedo Day • *US Naval Academy Day • Virgin Islands and Puerto Rico: Friendship Day • World Day Against the Death Penalty • *World Mental Health Day • Yorktown Victory Day

11. *Adding Machine Day • *General Pulaski Memorial Day • Ada Lovelace Day,*National Coming Out Day • Southern Food Heritage Day • United Nations: International Day of the Girl Child

12. Bahamas Discovery Day • Columbus Day (Traditional) • *Day of the Six–Billion • Emergency Nurses Day • Equatorial Guinea: Independence Day • *International Moment of Frustration Scream Day • Mexico: Dia de la Raza • National Bring Your Teddy Bear to Work Day • National Bullying Prevention Day • National Fossil Day • National Take Your Parents to Lunch Day • Spain: National Holiday

13. *Jesse Leroy Brown Day • *Navy Birthday • United Nations: International Day for Natural Disaster Reduction • Whitehouse Cornerstone Laid (1792)

14. *Be Bald and Be Free Day • Sound Barrier Broken (1947) • Supersonic Skydive Day (2012)

15. *Blind Americans Equality Day (formerly White Cane Safety Day) • Bridge Day • First Manned Flight (1783) • International Raw Milk Cheese Appreciation Day • National Grouch Day • Sweetest Day • United Nations: International Day of Rural Women • Yorktown Victory Day

16. Birth Control Day (1916) • Dictionary Day • Global Cat Day • Million Man March (1995) • United Nations: World Food Day • Noah Webster Day

17. Black Poetry Day • Jamaica: National Heroes Day • Evel Knievel Day • *Mulligan Day • *National Boss' Day (Observed) • National Playing Card Collection Day • San Francisco Earthquake (1989) • Shemini Atzeret • *United Nations: International Day for the Eradication of Poverty • Virgin Islands: Hurricane Thanksgiving Day

18. Azerbaijan: Independence Day • BBC Day • Canada: Persons Day (1929) • Comic Strip Day • Saint Luke: Feast Day • Simchat Torah • Water Pollution Control Day • *World Menopause Day

19. Alaska Day • Evaluate Your Life Day • Hagfish Day • LGBT Center Awareness Day • Missouri Day • Yorktown Surrender Day

20. John Dewey Day • Get Smart About Credit Day • Get to Know Your Customers Day (third Thursday of each quarter is set aside to get to know your customers even better) • Guatemala: Revolution Day • Kenya: Mashujaa Day • Miss America Rose Day

21. *Incandescent Lamp Day • National Mammography Day • Nobel Prize Day • Taiwan: Overseas Chinese Day

22. *International Stuttering Awareness Day

23. Cambodia: Peace Treaty Day • Hungary: Republic Day (Declares Independence) • *IPod Day • Mother-In-Law Day • National Mole Day • Swallows Depart from San Juan Capistrano • Thailand: Chulalongkorn Day

24. First Barrel Jump over Niagara Falls (1901) • India: Diwali (Deepavali) • New Zealand: Labor Day • Recycle Your Mercury Thermostat Day • United Nations Day • *United Nations: World Development Information Day • Zambia: Independence Day

25. First Female FBI Agents (1972) • Picasso Day • Saint Crispin's Day • Sourest Day • Taiwan: Retrocession Day

26. Austria: National Day • Birth of the Bab • Erie Canal Day • Gunfight at the O.K. Corral (1881) • Mule Day

27. Birth of Baha'u'llah • *Cranky Coworkers Day • *Navy Day • Saint Vincent and the Grenadines • and Turkmenistan: Independence Day • United Nations: World Day for Audiovisual Heritage • *Walt Disney Day

28. Childcare Superhero Day • Czech Republic: Independence Day • Frankenstein Friday • Greece: Ochi Day • *Saint Jude's Day • Statue of Liberty Dedication (1886)

29. *Internet Created (1969) • National Cat Day • Turkey: Republic Day

30. Checklists Day • *Create A Great Funeral Day • Devil's Night • European Union: Daylight Savings Time Ends • *Haunted Refrigerator Night • National Candy Corn Day • *Emily Post Day • *Reformation Sunday • "War of the Worlds" (1938) • World Audio Drama Day

31. *Books for Treats Day • "Car Talk" Day • *Halloween or All Hallows' Eve • Houdini Day • *Magic Day • Mount Rushmore Day • *National Knock–Knock Day • National UNICEF Day • Samhain • Taiwan: Chiang Kai-Shek Day • Trick or Treat or Beggar's Night • United Nations: World Cities Day

# Holiday Marketing Ideas

**Emotional Intelligence Awareness Month** — It wasn't until recently that I realized that Emotional Intelligence (EI) is a real thing. EI helps us use our own and others emotional information to guide our thinking and behavior. So basically, it is the ability to understand the way people feel and react.

One sure way to celebrate is to take the test. I have placed the link to some online sources in the appropriate appendix.

Communication skills, body language, and other similar topics are all issues that can be covered as you make your way through this month-long holiday. Events, social media posts, graphics, and tips are all wonderful opportunities to share on these subjects while branding your business.

Do you have a book on this or similar topics? For those authors who are up to the task, it's a fine time to get going on a blog or podcast tour. I know one group of authors who have a recently released book titled, Emotional Intelligence in Christ and my own book Presentational Skills for the Next Generation are fine examples of what a book club or presentation could discuss. You'll find the links to these two books in the appendix.

**Oct 2 National G.E.O. (Growth.Overcome.Empower)** — Wow, this weird & wacky holiday covers a plethora of subject matters! Business and personal, career and spiritual topics and all things related to them could expand your ability to reach a larger audience. Developing a business marketing or plan, overcoming bad habits, and learning new skills are all topics you could use in a live or online conference.

For the meek at heart, simply posting tips and graphics on social media is always an option. But I challenge you to step out of your comfort zone and overcome your fears to sponsor, host, or participate in a day-long event.

**Oct 5 Random Acts of Poetry Day** — Dust off your rhyming gene and share your poetry. Heck, it doesn't even have to rhyme! Were you aware that there isn't just one style of poetry? Sure enough, there are at least three that I can cite off the top of my head, and I'm not a poet. Yes, I have penned one or two in my time, okay three or four, but that doesn't make me a poet by any means. So, if I can offer up a poem or four, I am certain you can create one or two of your own to share on social media with your brand intact. Look in the appendix for a few facts about poetry that I was able to cull from the internet. Offer them as they are or as questions, it's your choice.

What would be even more fun would be to have a group poem writing session where everyone adds a line to create your group's unique poem. Another poetic idea would be to put together a poem anthology with your customers and friends. Give them a subject — or not — and let them loose with a pen and paper. Then you could hire a formatter and cover designer (shameless plug) and you'd have a poetry book you all could share.

Poetry by your favorite poets shared on social media or even facts about them could be fun as well. Don't forget to share their photos, if you can locate them, as we all know graphics attract more views on social media than a text post.

**Oct 8 Universal Music Day** — Gather a group of the musically inclined and contact your local nursing home or Hospice facility to let them know you and your group can come and sing or play a concert for their residents. If you make a day of it, you could do a tour of more than one institution. If you organize a few musical teams to participate, you may even be able to get some much-coveted press.

Alternatively, you may want to post lyrics as a guess this song title game on your social media. Better yet, make it an event and play some additional musically themed games to round out a melodically themed webinar. A couple of harmonious games you might consider are shared in the Samples Appendix.

**Oct 15 Bridge Day** — Span the great divide and share your brilliance today. Bridge the gap between fear and confidence with an event worthy webinar. Ask speakers to join you who can contribute on team, personal, and business building topics.

As your speakers promote the event, they will be introducing your business to their fans and thus increasing your reach to others who may end up hiring you or purchasing your products and/or services. We all understand what that could possibly do to your bottom line.

**Oct 28 Childcare Superhero Day** — Moms, dads, grandparents, and custodial caregivers share the need, for a time, to engage a childcare worker to attend to their children while they work. So, to thank them for their service, consider putting together a gift basket for them. When you contact other businesses in your local area and ask them to participate in your gift giving you may find you have enough to deliver baskets to one or more childcare services. They may even want to help you deliver them. If not, asking teenagers to assist you might be a wise choice. Be sure to let the media in your area know what you are doing, and you might just get the press' attention. Who knows, you may be asked to speak on a radio or TV show. We all know what that can do to bring attention to your business.

# NOVEMBER

Nov 21 – Dec 18 FOFA World Cup Qatar 2022
Nov 27 – Jan 6, 2022 Netherlands: Midwinter Horn Blowing

## Month-Long Holidays

American Diabetes Month • Aviation History Month • Banana Pudding Lovers Month • Diabetic Eye Disease Month • Eye Donation Month • Lung Cancer Awareness Month • Movember • National Adoption Month • National Epilepsy Awareness Month • National Family Caregivers Month • National Forgiveness and Happiness Day • National Georgia Pecan Month • National Inspirational Role Models Month • National Long-Term Care Awareness Month • National Marrow Awareness Month • National Memoir Writing Month • National Native American Heritage Month • National Novel Writing Month • National Runaway Prevention Month • Peanut Butter Lovers' Month • Picture Book Month • Prematurity Awareness Month • World Vegan Month • World Bereaved Siblings Awareness Month

## Week-Long Holidays

Nov 6 – 12 Polar Bear Week
Nov 14 – 18 American Education Week
Nov 18 – 24 World Antimicrobial Awareness Week (tentative)
Nov 20 – 26 National Family Week
Nov 11 – 13 National Donor Sabbath

## Daily Holidays

1. 1. Algeria: Revolution Day • *All Hallows or All Saints Day • Antigua and Barbuda: Independence Day • European Union Day (1993) • Extra Mile Day • Israel: Aliyah Day (Yom Ha'Aliyah) • Lisbon Earthquake (1755) • Mexico: Day of the Dead • *National Authors' Day • National Forgiveness and Happiness Day • National Sports Fan Day • US Virgin Islands: Liberty Day • World Vegan Day

2. *All Souls Day • Daniel Boone Day • *First Scheduled Radio Broadcast (1920) • National Broadcast Traffic Professionals Day • United Nations: International Day to End Impunity for Crimes Against Journalists

3. Canada: New Inuit Territory Approved (1992) • *Cliché Day • Dewey Day • Dominica: National Day • International Day Against Violence and Bullying at School, including Cyberbullying

(UNESCO) • *Japan: Culture Day • Micronesia and Panama: Independence Day • National Men Make Dinner Day • Public Television Day • *Sandwich Day • SOS Day

4. Fountain Pen Day • Italy: Victory Day • *King Tut Tomb Discovery (1922) • Mischief Night • National Easy Bake Oven Day • National Medical Science Liaison (MSL) Awareness and Appreciation Day • Panama: Flag Day • Russia: Unity Day • Samoa: Arbor Day • UNESCO Day

5. El Salvador: Day of the First Shout for Independence • *England: Guy Fawkes Day • Vivian Leigh—Scarlett O'Hara Day (1913) • National Bison Day • *Shattered Backboard Day • Sadie Hawkins Day • Sweden: All Saints' Day • United Nations: World Tsunami Awareness Day

6. Daylight Savings Time Ends: Standard Time Resumes • Morocco: Anniversary of the Green March • Saxophone Day • Sweden: Gustavus Adolphus Day • *United Nations: International Day for Preventing the Exploitation of the Environment in War and Armed Conflict • Zero Tasking Day

7. Australia: Recreation Day • Bangladesh: Solidarity Day • Madam Curie Day • Fill Our Staplers Day • First Black Governor Elected (1989) • Republican Symbol Day (1874) • Russia: Revolution Day

8. Abet and Aid Punsters Day • Cook Something Bold and Pungent Day • General Election Day • Shakespeare Authorship Mystery Day • *X–ray Day

9. *Berlin Wall Opened (1989) • Boston Fire (1872) • Cambodia: Independence Day • East Coast Blackout (1965) • Germany: Kristallnacht • National Child Safety Council Day • Vietnam Veterans Memorial Statue Unveiling (1984)

10. *Area Code Day (1951) • Marine Corps Day • Panama: First Shout of Independence • Return Day • Sesame Street Anniversary (1969) • United Nations: World Science Day for Peace and Development

11. Angola: Independence Day • *Bonza Bottler Day™ • Canada: Remembrance Day • China: Singles Day • Columbia: Cartagena Independence Day • Death/Duty Day • England: Remembrance Day • God Bless America Day • Japan: Origami Day • Maldives: Republic Day • Poland: Independence Day • Sweden: Saint Martin's Day • Switzerland: Martinmas Goose (Martinigians) • Veterans Day (1919) • WWI Armistice Day

12. Mexico: Postman's Day • World Pneumonia Day

13. Germany: Volkstrauertag • Holland Tunnel Day

14. Dow Jones Tops 1,000 (1642) • Guinea-Bissau: Readjustment Movement's Day • India: Children's Day • International Day Against Illicit Trafficking in Cultural Property (UNESCO) • Loosen Up Lighten Up Day • Moby Dick Day • Claude Monet Day • National Block It Out Day • *United Nations: World Diabetes Day

15. *America Recycles Day • Belgium: Dynasty Day • Brazil: Republic Day • George Spelvin Day • National Bundt Day

16. Estonia: Day of National Rebirth • Germany: Buss und Bettag • *Lewis and Clark Expedition Reaches Pacific Ocean (1805) • National Educational Support Professionals Day • Saint Eustatius, West Indies: Statia and America Day • *United Nations: International Day for Tolerance

17. Great American Smoke-out (third Thursday) • *Homemade Bread Day • National Unfriend Day • Suez Canal Day • World Philosophy Day • World Prematurity Day

18. Haiti: Army Day • International Day of Islamic Art (UNESCO) • Latvia: Independence Day • Married to a Scorpio Support Day • Mickey Mouse Day • Oman: National Holiday • Substitute Educators Day • US Uniform Time Zone Plan Day

19. Belize: Garifuna Day • Cold War Ends (1990) • *Dedication Day (1862) • First Automatic Toll Collection Machine (1954) • Gandhi Day • Garfield Day • *"Have A Bad Day" Day • Monaco: National Holiday • Puerto Rico: Discovery Day • Thailand: Elephant Roundup at Surin • United Nations: World Toilet Day

20. *Bill of Rights Day • Edwin Powell Hubble Day • Germany: Totensonntag • *Mandelbrot Day (1924) • Mexico: Revolution Day • *Name Your PC Day • Stir Up Sunday • Transgender Day of Remembrance • *United Nations: African Industrialization Day • United Nations: Universal Children's Day • United Nations: World Day of Remembrance for Road Traffic Victims

21. *United Nations: World Television Day • World Hello Day

22. Charles De Gaulle Day 1890) • *George Eliot (1819) • Lebanon: Independence Day • Edward Teach "Blackbeard" Death (1718)

23. Billy the Kid Day • Fibonacci Day • Israel: Sigid • Japan: Labor Thanksgiving Day • Boris Karloff Day • Harpo Marx Day

24. *Dale Carnegie (1888) • *Celebrate Your Unique Talent Day • *D.B. Cooper Day • Tie One On Day™ • Thanksgiving Day

25. Black Friday • Bosnia and Herzegovina: National Day • Buy Nothing Day (25–26) • *Andrew Carnegie (1835) • Dine Over Your Kitchen Sink Day • Family Day in Nevada • *JFK Day (1960) • National Flossing Day • Native American Heritage Day • Saint Catherine's Day • Suriname: Independence Day • United Nations: International Day for the Elimination of Violence Against Women Day

26. Alice in Wonderland Day • International Aura Awareness Day • Mongolia: Republic Day • Charles Schultz (1922) • Small Business Saturday • World Olive Tree Day

27. Advent First Sunday • Artists Sunday® • Face Transplant Day • Handel's Messiah Sing-Along Day • Laerdal Tunnel Opening (2000) • Bruce Lee Day • Slinky™ Day

28. *Albania: Independence Day • Chad: Republic Day • Cider Monday • Cyber Monday • *Lévi Strauss (1908) • Mauritania: Independence Day • Panama: Independence from Spain

29. Alcott Day • Czechoslovakia Ends Communist Rule (1989) • *Electronic Greetings Day • Giving Tuesday • *CS Lewis (1898) • *United Nations: International Day of Solidarity with the Palestinian People

30. Articles of Peace Between Great Britain and the US (1782) • Barbados: Independence Day • Computer Security Day • Philippines: Bonifacio Day • Saint Andrew's Day • *Stay Home Because You're Well Day • United Nations: Day of Remembrance for all Victims of Chemical Warfare

# Holiday Marketing Ideas

**National Inspirational Role Models Month** — If you have ever wanted to participate in a mentorship program, now is your chance to do just that. Whether you decide to go it alone or join an existing mentorship program you will be glad you did. Some mentors I have heard from say that they grew as much — if not more — than those whom they mentored.

If you aren't sure how to start a mentorship program you need to look no further than the 2013 Weird & Wacky Holiday Marketing Guide. Look for the topic, "Mentoring Tips from the Experts" in the Samples Appendix.

**Nov 3 SOS Day** — The most obvious way to celebrate this holiday is to get in contact with your customers and clients and ask them if they have any questions or concerns that you can address. They may have a surprising suggestion that will open your mind to a product or service you hadn't thought of before. Perhaps it will be just something that needs improving upon. Whatever they say, take it to heart because if one person is saying it many more are thinking it.

Even if they don't have any suggestions or comments, you at least have reminded them that you are still in business. Then, when they or their contacts have a need for your services, you'll be top on their list.

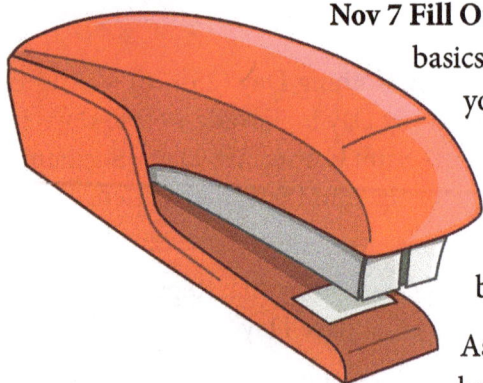

**Nov 7 Fill Our Staplers Day** — This is a reminder to ensure your basics are covered. If you need to replenish your stock or even your own self, today is the time to get it done.

The first way you can use this day to promote your business is to send a notecard, email, or make a phone call to your customers and clients thanking them for being 'a staple to your business' success'.

As you consider how to help others replenish their storehouses, why not share stress relief or business building tips? These are the basic essentials for every entrepreneur. This can be done with simple social media posts or graphics that you have branded to your business. I have placed one in the appendix that you can alter to fit your brand identity.

Alternatively, you might entertain the idea of hosting an event. You could invite speakers who can share on any number of business building topics such as how to write a business proposal (this is not the same thing as a business plan, but you could offer that too) • record keeping, maximizing sales with easy to implement tracking tools, and much more.

**Nov 11 Bonza Bottler Day**™ — If you are a fan of the Weird & Wacky Holiday Marketing Guide, you already know all about this weird & wacky holiday. If not, you are in for a treat. Every month as a BBD in that the month and days that repeat, like today's 11/11. This holiday is all about having fun! Just get out there and have a relaxing good time with family and friends, co-workers, or clients. It's your party and you can invite whomever you choose. You know what they say about all work and no play . . .

**Nov 14 National Block It Out Day** — Truthfully, there are two ways to 'block it out'. One is to ignore the problem and the other is to solve it. Blocking it out gets me thinking about meditation, EFT Tapping, and sunglasses. I know, sunglasses, right, but there is eye care and fashion that evolves from eye protection.

As for solving the problem, well just about any subject you can think of can be overcome with a little instruction from one who has gone before.

Both of these ways of handling challenges can be addressed in a comprehensive event. You might even launch your coaching program today!

**Nov 20 Stir Up Sunday** — While the reason for this weird & wacky holiday is about cooking, I see this as a marketing opportunity by shaking things up a bit. Yes, a social media campaign wishing a happy holiday, or even sharing your favorite recipes is an easy answer. I've shared a couple of my favorite recipes which you'll find in the appendix.

However, to make it worth your effort why not consider some other options? Could it mean exercise training or tips? Or maybe you could invite others mastermind with you. It's your choice, as always, but the more involved you are the longer your reach will become.

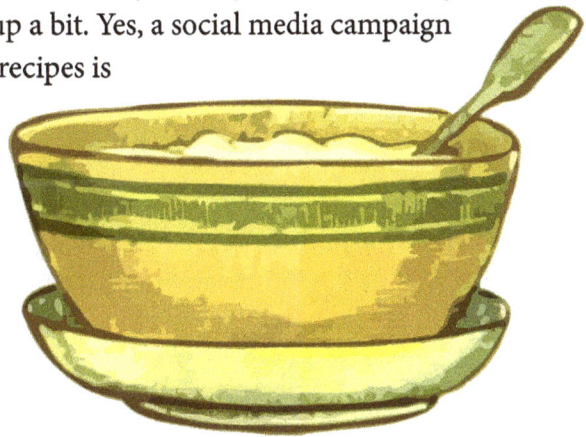

Nov 30 Computer Security Day — If you own a computer security company then you have a built-in weird & wacky holiday that fits your business to a tee. If not, then you might need to think of a different spin to your drive.

Perhaps you could invite a local security pro to speak to your customers and clients. Another alternative could be to share tips on how to secure more online business opportunities. That could include marketing, planning, communication skills, and public speaking to name a few. Better yet, make a day of it and host an event!

I've mentioned it before and will again. Events are the best way to market your business. Whether you host the event, sponsor it, or just present, events are the marketing tool that you should definitely have securely in your marketing plan.

# DECEMBER

Dec 14 – Jan 5, 2022 Christmas Bird Count

Dec 14 – 28 Halcyon Days

Dec 15 – Jan 6, 2022 Puerto Rico: Navidades

Dec 16 – 24 Mexico: Posadas

Dec 19 – 26 Chanukah

Dec 26 – Jan 1 Kwanzaa

## Month-Long Holidays

Bingo's Birthday Month • Give the Gift of Sight Month • National Impaired Driving Prevention Month • National Write a Business Plan Month • Worldwide Food Service Safety Month

## Week-Long Holidays

Dec 5 – 9 Older Driver Safety Awareness Week

Dec 10 – 17 Human Rights Week

Dec 17 – 23 Saturnalia

## Daily Holidays

1. Antarctica Day • *Basketball Day • *Bifocals at the Monitor Liberation Day • Canada: Yukon Order of Pioneers (1894) • *Civil Air Patrol Day • Portugal: Independence Day • Romania: National Holiday • Rosa Parks Day • *United Nations: World AIDS Day

2. *Artificial Heart Transplant Day (1967) • *Joseph Bell (1837) • England: Walter Plinge Day • Ghana: National Farmers' Day • Laos: National Day • National Mutt Day—December • National Sales Person's Day • *Special Education Day • United Arab Emirates: Independence Day • *United Nations: International Day for the Abolition of Slavery Day

3. Be a Blessing Day • First Heart Transplant (1967) • *United Nations: International Day of Persons with Disabilities

4. *Samuel Butler (1835) • Mary Celeste Discovery Day • National Grange Day • Saint Barbara's Day • United Nations: International Day of Banks

5. *AFL–CIO Founded (1955) • Austria: Krampuslauf • *Bathtub Party Day • Central African Republic: National Day (observed) • Christmas to Remember Day • *Walt Disney (1901) • Haiti: Discovery Day • "Irrational Exuberance" Day • Montgomery Bus Boycott Remembrance Day •

*United Nations: International Volunteer Day for Economic and Social Development • United Nations: World Soil Day

6. Ecuador: Day of Quito: Founding (1534) • Everglades National Park Established (1947) • Finland: Independence Day • Missouri Earthquakes (1811) • *National Miners' Day • *National Pawnbrokers Day • *Saint Nicholas Day • Spain: Constitution Day

7. Armenian Earthquake (1988) • Cote D'Ivoire: Commemoration Day • Iran: Students Day • *National Fire Safety Council Day (1979) • *National Pearl Harbor Remembrance Day • Special Kids Day • *United Nations: International Civil Aviation Day

8. AFL Day • Feast of Immaculate Conception • Guam: Lady of Camarin Day • Intermediate-Range Nuclear Forces Treaty (INF) Signed (1987) • NAFTA Day • National Lard Day • Soviet Union Dissolved (1991) • Uzbekistan: Constitution Day • *Eli Whitney (1765)

9. Birdseye Day • Official Lost and Found Day • Tanzania: Independence and Republic Day • *United Nations: International Anti-Corruption Day • United Nations: International Day of Commemoration and Dignity of the Victims of the Crime of Genocide and of the Prevention of this Crime

10. Jane Addams Day • *Dewey Decimal System Day • *Emily Dickinson (1830) • Encyclopedia Britannica First Published (1879) • *Thomas Hopkins Gallaudet (1787) • *Human Rights Day • *Ada Lovelace (1815) • National Day of the Horse,*Nobel Prize Awards Ceremonies • Thailand: Constitution Day • *United Nations: Human Rights Day

11. Burkino Faso: Independence Day • Kaleidoscope Day • *UNICEF Birthday • *United Nations: International Mountain Day

12. *Bonza Bottler Day™ • Day of Our Lady of Guadalupe • Kenya: Jamhuri Day (Independence Day) • Mexico: Guadalupe Day • *Poinsettia Day • *Puerto Rico: Las Mañanitas • Turkmenistan: Neutrality Day • United Nations: International Day of Neutrality • United Nations: International Universal Health Coverage Day

13. China: Nanking Massacre Memorial Day • Malta: Republic Day • *New Zealand Discovery Day (1642) • Sweden: Saint Lucia Day

14. *Doolittle Day • Nostradamus (1503) • South Pole Discovery (1911)

15. *Bill of Rights Day • *Cat Herders Day • Curaçao: Kingdom Day and Antillean Flag Day

16. *Jane Austen (1775) • Bahrain: Independence Day • Bangladesh: Victory Day • *Barbie and Barney Backlash Day • *Ludwig Van Beethoven (1770) • Boston Tea Party Day • Kazakhstan: Independence Day • Philippines: Philippine Christmas Observance and Simbang Gabi • South Africa: Reconciliation Day • Underdog Day • *United Nations: Revokes Resolution on Zionism (1991)

17. *Aztec Calendar Stone Discovery Day (1790) • *Clean Air Day • First Flight Anniversary Celebration Day • *Joseph Henry (1797) • Libby Day • *Wright Brothers Day

18. FOFA World Cup Final • Chanukah (begins at sundown) • *Benjamin O Davis, Jr. (1912) • *Joseph Grimaldi (1778) • Mexico: Feast of Our Lady of Solitude • Niger: Republic Day • Take a New Year's Resolution to Stop Smoking (TANYRSS) Day • "To Tell the Truth" Day • United Nations: Arabic Language Day • *United Nations: International Migrants Day

19. Titanic Day

20. American Poet Laureate Day • Montgomery Bus Boycott Ends (1956) • *Mudd Day • *United Nations: International Human Solidarity Day

21. *Heinrich Böll (1917) • Celebrate Short Fiction Day • *Crossword Puzzle Day • Benjamin Disraeli Birth (1804) • *Forefathers Day • *Humbug Day • *Phileas Fogg Win a Wager Day • Pilgrim Landing • Shorts Day (Shake and Freeze Day) • United Kingdom Allows Same-Sex Civil Partnerships Day • Yalda • Yule

22. Be a Lover of Silence Day • First Gorilla Born in Captivity (1956) • Oglethorpe Day • *Giacomo Puccini (1858)

23. *Federal Reserve System (1913) • Festivus • First Non-stop Flight Around the World (1987) • Metric Conversion Act (1975) • Mexico: Feast of Radishes • *Transistor Day (1947)

24. Austria: "Silent Night, Holy Night" • *Christmas Eve • First Surface-to-Surface Guided Missile • *James Prescott Joule (1818) • Libya: Independence Day

25. *A'Phabet Day or No-L-Day • *Christmas Day • Cuba: Christmas Returns • Taiwan: Constitution Day • Washington Crosses the Delaware (1776)

26. *Bahamas: Junkanoo • Boxing Day • Laurent Clerc Day (1795) • Ireland: Day of the Wren • Luxembourg: Blessing of the Wine • National Candy Cane Day • *National Whiner's Day • Radium Discovery Day • Saint Stephen's Day • Second Day of Christmas • Slovenia: Independence Day • South Africa: Day of Goodwill • United Kingdom: Boxing Day

27. "Howdy Doody" Day • *Johannes Kepler (1571) • *Louis Pasteur (1822) • Radio City Music Hall Day • Saint John Feast Day • United Kingdom: Christmas Holiday (Substitute) • United Nations: International Day of Epidemic Preparedness

28. Australia: Proclamation Day • *Cinema Day • Endangered Species Day • *Holy Innocents Day or Childermas • *Pledge of Allegiance Day

29. "Butterfly Effect" Day • Andrew Johnson Wreath-Laying • Saint Thomas of Canterbury: Feast Day • *Tick Tock Day • *YMCA Day

30. *Falling Needles Family Fest Day • *Rudyard Kipling (1865) • "Let's Make a Deal" Day • No Interruptions Day • Philippines: Rizal Day • USSR Day (1922)

31. First US Bank Opens (1781) • *First Nights • *Japan: Namahage • *Leap Second Adjustment Time Day • *Make Up Your Mind Day • *New Year's Eve • Saint Sylvester's Day • Scotland: Hogmany

## Holiday Marketing Ideas

**Give the Gift of Sight Month**—Gather a group of colleagues and help promote eye doner awareness. One way to do this is with a signature drive. Contact your nearest eye bank, they may be of help in promoting your efforts as well as instructing you on how to organize your drive according to their requirements. Some may even share stories from recipient and donors in the case you host an event. Either of these two choices deserves a bit of media attention. So, be sure to let them know.

Did you know you don't have to be dead to donate your eye? Facts like this about eye care could be easily shared on social media. Be sure to brand your graphics when you create them. You can find an infographic I designed that you could brand and use as you wish in the appendix as well as a list of facts you can use in your promotional efforts.

*Illustration 43718964 | Blessed Cartoon Text © Dawn Hudson | Dreamstime.com*

**Dec 3 Be a Blessing Day** — While you make your way through this special day spread happiness and cheer along your path. Offer a kind word when spoken to, send a card or note to your customers and clients who have proven to be your most loyal, or merely share your smile with everyone you meet as you wish them a happy Be a Blessing Day.

Pay it forward is a wonderful movement that you could embrace today. Share your goodwill with others today as you hand out your business card, attached to a simple gift of a small individually wrapped candy. In keeping with the season, it could be a candy cane or even a chocolate kiss, if you want to get decadent, you could share a Werther's candy or something even more elaborate.

Here's an idea that you could do that might endear you to the press. Ask some local companies to sponsor you or your team. Then purchase small stuffed animals in bulk and take them to your local children's hospital to give out to the kids. Be sure to check with the hospital to make sure that stuffed animals are okay to give. If not, you will have to bulk purchase something that is approved.

For preemies they have strict guidelines, but for the older children they may be much more accepting of your idea.

Don't forget to let your local press know what you are doing. At the very least take a short video to share on social media. If it goes viral, you may end up garnering the attention of the national media. How cool would that be?

**Dec 9 Official Lost and Found Day** — There are a couple of really fine ideas you can use to promote your business today. The first that comes to mind is to go through your old client list and contact them to let you know they are on your mind. You might use the time with them to let them know what new products and services you offer. However, be sure to keep it a friendly chat and not all about business.

The second idea is to host an event that covers subjects that help others find solutions to their issues. You could do this as just a mastermind session or you could make it a full-blown seminar/webinar. When you schedule the latter, your speakers will help get the word out to their customers and clients, therefore broadening your reach.

**Dec 11 Kaleidoscope Day**—While looking through the lens offering colorful insight into your business, today could be a terrific time to reflect on your business' potential for a whole new spectrum of ideas! Opportunities abound as you begin your marketing and business growth for the upcoming year. Consider spending time with your customers and clients to discover how you can help them reach their goals for the new year or simply focus on your own.

As always, social media and events are wonderfully exciting and fun ways to share your branded wishes for this weird & wacky holiday. To assist you in scheduling your event I have designed a Kaleidoscope Day event flyer which you will, of course, find in the appendix.

**Dec 26 National Whiner's Day**—To finish off 2022 on a high note for your business, National Whiner's Day comes to your rescue. Again, touching base with your customers and clients who haven't done business with you recently will help you to uncover any issues they may have and help to solve them. It doesn't necessarily have to be about problems they have with your business, it could just be about helping them refocus on ways to overcome their challenges. If you are a coach, of any kind, this is a superb concept for you to utilize today.

Alternatively, you might host or sponsor an event touching on how to stop whining and act. Attitude, communication, and conflict resolution could all be viable topics to share in your event. As you already know, events are the most effective advertising tool and the key to many business successes. So, don't shy away from hosting or sponsoring events. Instead embrace them wholeheartedly and watch your client base and bottom-line increase in the years to come.

# Appendix A: SAMPLES

## Sample Press Release

**FOR IMMEDIATE RELEASE**

**30+ YEAR LOCAL VETERAN BUSINESS OWNER / AUTHOR PARTNERS WITH PNC BANK**

### CLEARWATER, FL— SEPTEMBER 21, 2014

Local author and publisher, Ginger Marks, partners with Clearwater's PNC Bank to provide insight and advice for prospective, new, and experienced business owners. Ginger will be available to chat and sign copies of her award-winning book, Complete Library of Entrepreneurial Wisdom and PNC Financial experts will be on hand to field your questions and educate you on business financial matters.

Mrs. Marks has spent 30+ years in the Tampa Bay area honing her skill as an entrepreneur. Having owned and operated multiple businesses, including a restaurant and a multimillion-dollar surgical clinic, she knows her way around business and how to operate one successfully.

Mrs. Marks states, "Owning a business takes many talents and the determination to succeed. In the course of my business operations I have experienced both the ups and the downs of the financial market. Without the knowledge of how to structure your finances to support your dreams you endanger your success. This is why I have partnered with PNC with the release of this important work."

Event date and location: October 9, 2014 between 5:30 and 6:30 pm at 2498 Gulf-to-Bay Blvd. Books available at your local bookstore and at this event.

# # #

MEDIA CONTACT: Ginger Marks, ginger.marks@documeantdesings.com 1 (727) 565–2100.

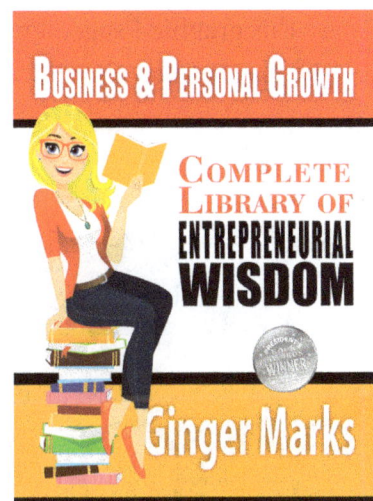

# International Clean-Up Your Computer Day Infographic

Courtesy of Wondershare.com

To use this graphic I suggest you piece these two pages together, or email me and I'll be happy to send you the file. You can also download it from Wondershare.com.

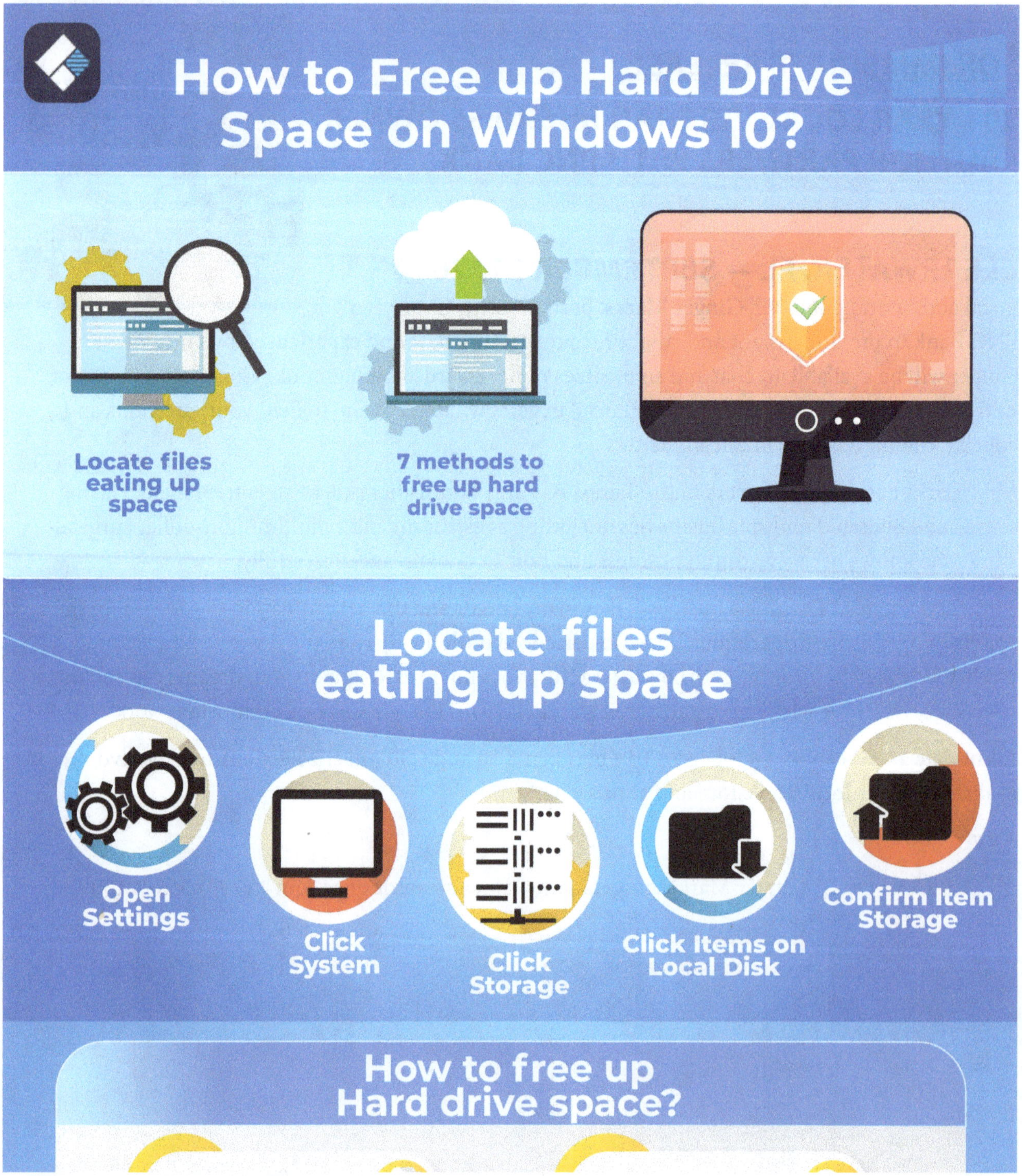

## How to Free up Hard Drive Space on Windows 10?

Locate files eating up space

7 methods to free up hard drive space

## Locate files eating up space

Open Settings

Click System

Click Storage

Click Items on Local Disk

Confirm Item Storage

## How to free up Hard drive space?

**Open Settings**

**Click System**

**Click Storage**

**Click Items on Local Disk**

**Confirm Item Storage**

# How to free up Hard drive space?

**01** Delete Junk Files

**02** Remove Temporary Files

**03** Uninstall Apps & Games

**04** Migrate Files to External Hard Drive

**05** Store Files onto Cloud

**06** Disable Hibernation

**07** Compress Windows 10 Installation

# Accidentally delete important data during the cleanup?

**Wondershare Recoverit**

- Recover data easily in three simple steps
- Retrieve data safely from crashed computer
- Repair corrupted videos professionally

# Joygerm Mini-Candy Bar Wrappers

For full size graphic contact Ginger at designer@DocUmeantDesigns.com

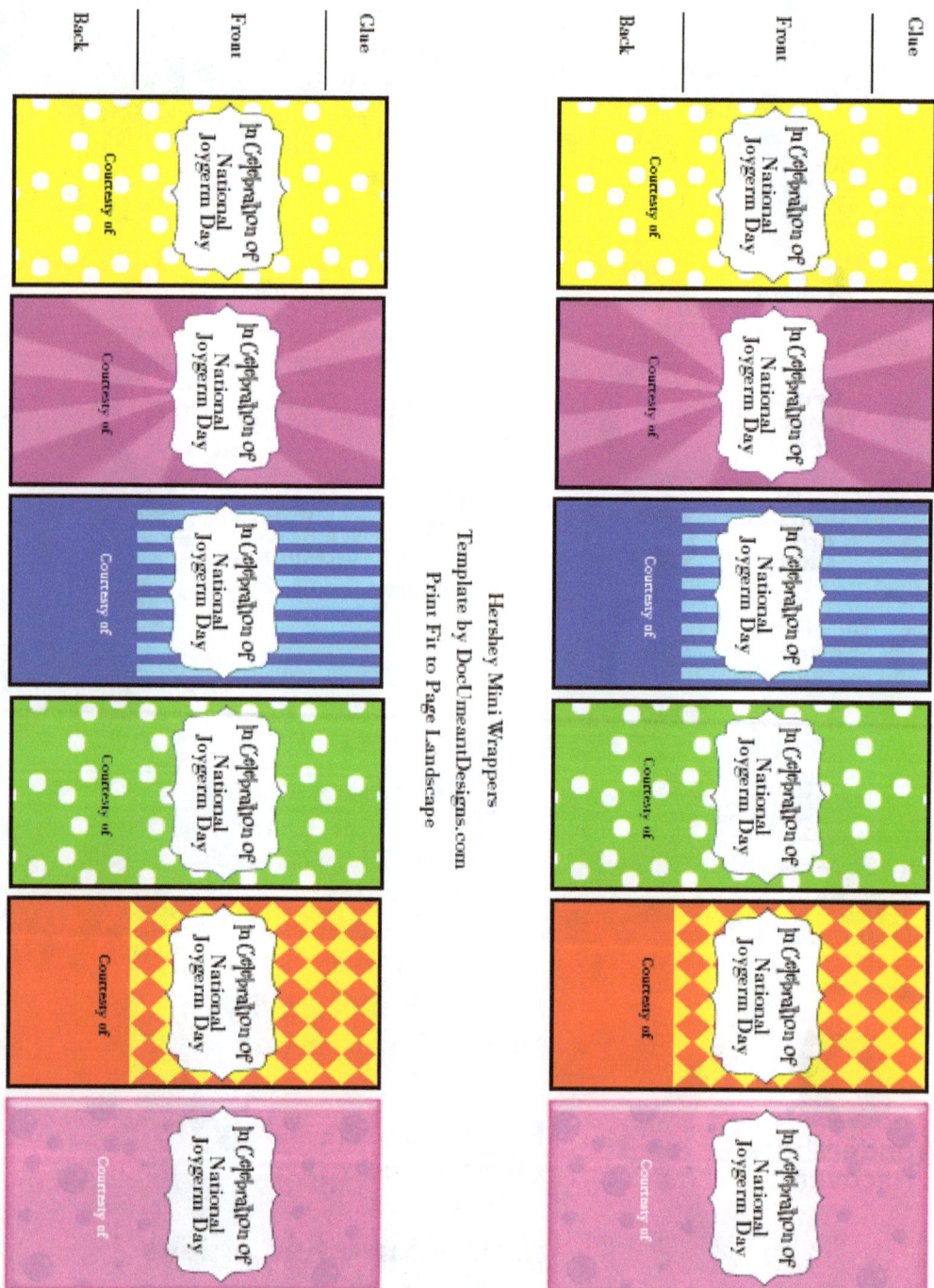

Hershey Mini Wrappers
Template by DocUmeantDesigns.com
Print Fit to Page Landscape

Glue

Front

Back

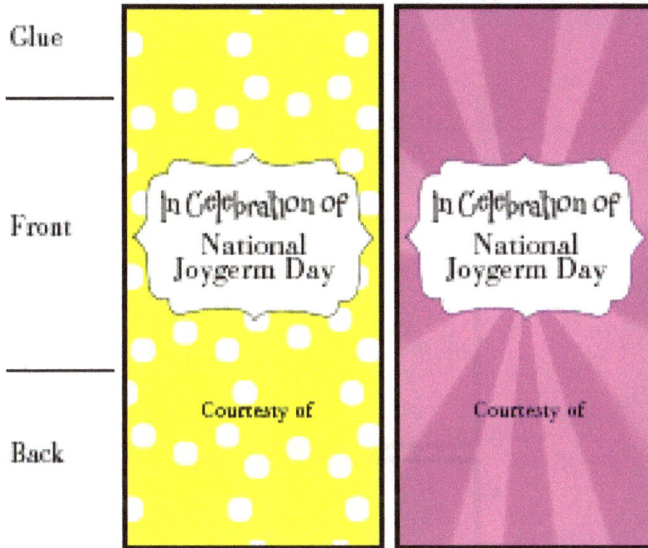

Glue

Front

Back

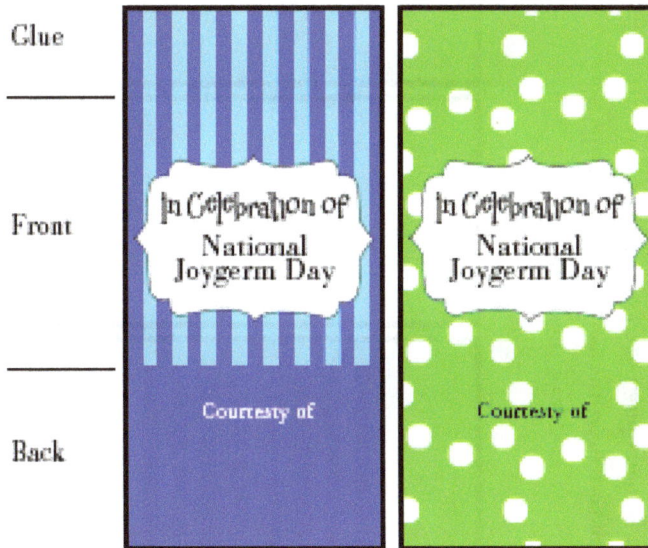

Glue

Front

Back

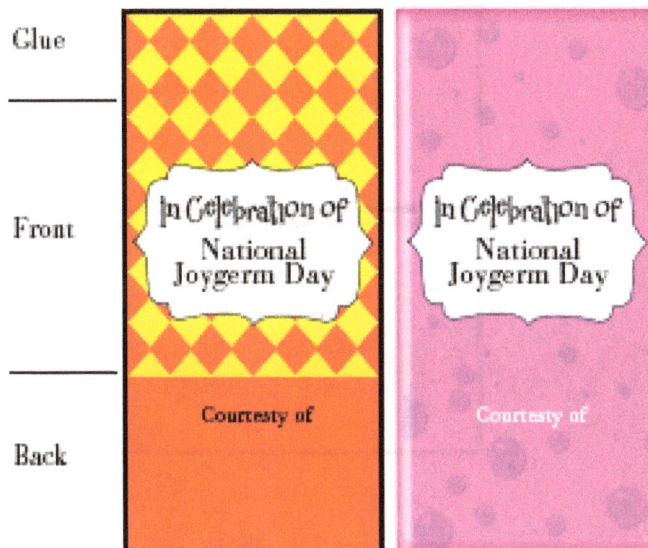

I have provided this blank template for your creative freedom.

Back | Front | Glue          Back | Front | Glue

Hershey Mini Wrappers
Template by DocUmeantDesigns.com
Print Fit to Page Landscape

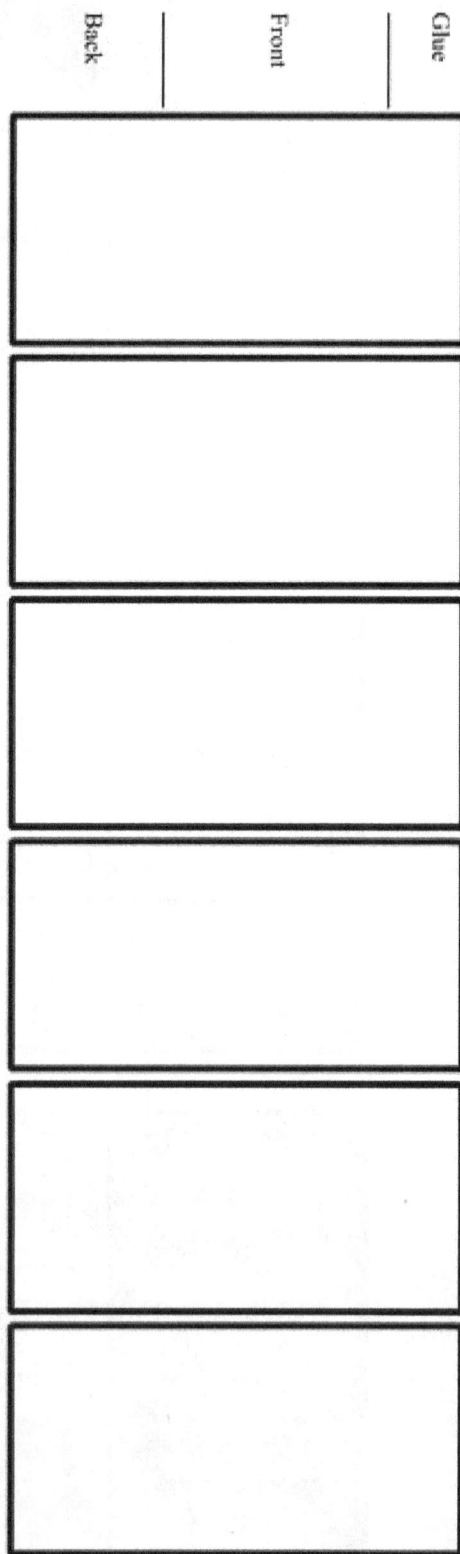

# National Medal of Honor Day

Designed by DocUmeant Designs

**Instructions:**

Change colors to match company brand.

Place company logo in center circle.

Save as gif, png, or tif.

Share with your most loyal, or all, of your customers/clients.

# Memory Games

## Match Game

## Instructions:

Create a branded match game by drawing or pasting pictures—perhaps using your products or service names—on cardstock. Place plain black or brand colored squares over each picture and glue top only to cardstock over each picture.

Hand one out to each participant.

## Directions:

The principle of the game is to find all the pairs by returning the cards 2 by 2. If the cards turned up are the same (a pair), it's a match and you win the pair, otherwise, the cards are turned face down again and you have to make a new match.

Set a time limit to solve or first one to match all wins.

This game is best played in person, as internet speed could be a factor when played online.

*The following games are provided by All American Homecare*

## Words Association Games

This game is very well-known and quite simple. Nevertheless, it's still one of the most useful memory games for elderly people. Quick guidelines for those who do not remember the rules (though they may vary from company to company). Let's say, you play this game with your grandmother. One of you says the first word, for example, "flame". Your grandmother should say the word that she associates with the word flame, like "heat". Then it's your turn again, and you say "central heating". And so, it goes until you get tired of it.

This game allows people to build associative chains, to remember the words and their meaning. Also, if played in a large group of individuals, it helps to spark communication by giving you topics for a discussion.

## Words

Pretty similar to the previous activity, although it's a bit different. Players just keep saying the words one by one. The thing is you have to say a word that starts with the same letter that the previous word ends with. The main goal of this memory game for seniors is to boost their memories. Your elderly relative has to remember a lot of words and keep in mind which ones were already used.

## PUZZLE GAMES FOR SENIORS

For many people, puzzles were the very first game to train their minds. As we age, we may forget how effective it is. One of the key advantages of puzzles is that by composing pictures from numerous details, older people relax, their blood pressure decreases, and their breathing normalizes. For some people, this activity is something like meditation, so it's especially suitable for restless grandparents.

# BRAIN GAMES FOR SENIOR CITIZENS

Below there are special exercises for memory and attention — vital skills for seniors that can be lost without proper stimulation:

Name two items for each letter of your name. A more difficult task is to pick up five items for each letter without repeating.

Name all the months of the year in alphabetical order.

Name six or more items with the letter "C" that you can put on.

Carefully examine your surroundings for two minutes and try to find five red items that can be put in your pocket and five blue items that are too large for that.

Do not get disappointed if your relative fails to complete these tasks. It is not about winning here it is about giving the brain regular exercises.

## Sudoku

Sudoku is a great logical game for people of any age and with any abilities. It teaches you how to solve problems and find patterns in a series of numbers. The skills learned from playing Sudoku will be useful in everyday life: with their help, grandparents will be able to assess the consequences of the decisions they make every day. In addition, this is quite a difficult task, so a successfully solved Sudoku is a great achievement — and for elderly people, such achievements are the source of joy and a feeling of capability. Isn't that important?

# BOARD GAMES FOR SENIORS

One more type of mind game for seniors is board games. They are good for communication skills, attentiveness, memory, and much more.

## Chess

This game of strategists is very old. Since ancient times people knew that chess helps to sharpen the mind. It trains the most important skills — strategy building, planning, and non-standard thinking. In other words, this is a great activity for people of all ages.

Another advantage of this perfect board game for the elderly will be especially vital for older people, who find it difficult to focus, is that playing chess improves concentration.

# CARD GAMES FOR ELDERLY PEOPLE

Card games have been humanity's favorite for many centuries now. They are interesting, often unpredictable, they excite people and bring out their competitive spirit. Talking health-wise, card games help to improve motor skills and memory, as well as socialize. Also, many complicated memory card games for adults require full concentration and even calculation, all of which are a great help to the aging brain.

### Bridge

This game is not easy for those who have no idea how to play it, however, if your grandparents already have some experience with it, playing bridge with their friends will do them a lot of good! This game requires a lot of attention and thinking. Moreover, there are four players in the game, which means more communication!

### Poker

The world-famous card game will help your seniors to be excited and enthusiastic. They can invite their friends over for the tournament, which will give them plenty of socialization, not to mention the benefits of playing the game itself! Concentrate, remember, calculate, take a risk – all of these things give plenty of joy to your elders. And joy is very important for their mental health.

## GAMES FOR SENIORS WITH DEMENTIA

At All American Home Care, we offer many exercises and games for our seniors with dementia that not only stimulate their cognitive abilities (memory, attention, language, reasoning, etc.) but also have a positive effect on their emotional state and self-esteem. The best therapy is to spend time with them, surround them with the necessary love, care, understanding, and help them feel useful and important.

## Object Classification

Ask a relative with dementia to classify objects. For example, you can ask him to put things in order in a box, with buttons to arrange them by color or size. For this exercise, you can also use foods such as vegetables, fruits, berries, or herbs, or small items such as balls, pebbles, shells, etc. These activities will stimulate executive functions, abstraction, and reasoning.

## Board Games

Board games are great allies for stimulating the cognitive functions of relatives with dementia, as well as helping to have a good time with the family. Play dominoes, checkers, or monopoly. Of course, the types of games should not be too complex. Choose games that are adapted to your family's capabilities. All of your relatives should understand the rules and enjoy the process. If the standard rules of the game seem too complicated, you can always simplify them and develop your own rules that will be clear to each player.

# National Humor Month Jokes

Optimist: The glass is half full. Pessimist: The glass is half empty.
Mother: Why didn't you use a coaster!

What goes through every village, over mountains, crosses rivers and deserts and yet never moves?
A road.

A recent scientific study showed that out of 2,293,618,367 people, 94% are too lazy to actually read that number.

I've always thought my neighbors were quite nice people. But then they put a password on their Wi-Fi.

Q: Is Google male or female?
A: Female, because it doesn't let you finish a sentence before making a suggestion.

Q: Did you hear about the painter who was hospitalized?
A: They said he had too many strokes.

Q: Why did the cross-eyed teacher lose their job?
A: It was reported that she couldn't control her pupils?

Q: What do you call a cow with a twitch?
A: Beef Jerky.

Q: Can February March?
A: No, but April May.

Q: Why is basketball such a sloppy sport?
A: Because you dribble all over the floor.

Q: What do you get when you plant kisses?
A: Tu-lips.

Q: What is the best day to go to the beach?
A: Sun-day, of course!

Q: What's easy to get into, but hard to get out of?
A: Trouble.

Q: What kind of lights did Noah use on the ark?
A: Arc lights and floodlights.

Q: What's the difference between a teacher and a train?
A: The teacher says, "Spit out your gum," the trains says, "Chew, chew, chew".

Q: What is the longest word in the English language?
A: Smiles. Because there is a 'mile' between the s's.

Q: When's the best time to see a dentist?
A: Tooth-hurty.

Q: How many people can you fit in an empty VW?
A: One. After that it isn't empty?

Q: Which rock group has four guys but can't sing?
A: Mount Rushmore.

And my all-time favorite ...

Q: What did the green grape say to the blue grape?
A: OMG!!!! BREATHE!! BREATHE!!!

# How to Start a Mastermind Group

**Step 1:** Understand what a mastermind group is. In Napoleon Hill's *Think and Grow Rich*, he describes a mastermind group as "The coordination of knowledge and effort of two or more people, who work toward a definite purpose, in the spirit of harmony."

**Step 2:** Know your 'why'. Here's a short list that might help you along your journey.

1. Mutual support
2. Differing perspectives
3. Diverse resources or skillset
4. Accountability

**Step 3:** Invite members who will be committed to attending meet ups. They should have a similar drive to each other, have a diverse skill set, and be problem solvers. The best number of members for a well-established mastermind group is between three and five people.

**Step 4:** Set your parameters. Decide when, where, and how often you plan to meet. Divide the speaker's time equally among members. Determine if interruptions will be acceptable or strict, 'wait your turn' rules will be required. Decide if you want to have an agenda or open discussions, and whether or not your meetings will be recorded.

Consider, carefully, these five essential rules to building a successful mastermind group.

1. Choose Your Members Wisely
2. Set Ground Rules Immediately
3. Have a Clear Agenda & Structure for Each Meeting
4. Decide Upon a Group Leader
5. Share Evenly

**Step 5:** Start your meeting with a couple of essential questions, What are you working on? And What do you need help with? You might also ask them to share what they accomplished or learned since the last meeting.

# Tips On the Health Benefits of Proper Foot Care

## Basic Tips

Check them daily for cuts, sores, swelling, and infected toenails.

Give them a good cleaning in warm water but avoid soaking them because that may dry them out.

Moisturize them every day with lotion, cream, or petroleum jelly. Alternatively, you could wear special socks and lotion at bedtime.

## Don'ts

Avoid wearing tight-fitting shoes.

Skip the flip-flops and flats.

Don't share shoes.

Don't hide discolored nails with polish. Let them breathe and treat the underlying issue.

Don't shave calluses.

## Do's

Do try the Legs-Up-the-Wall yoga pose after a long day or a hard workout.

Do give yourself a foot massage or book a reflexology session.

Do roll a tennis ball under your feet.

Do soothe irritation with a vinegar foot soak.

Do repair, recycle, or toss when appropriate.

Wear only cloth shoes for leisure activities.

Wear sneakers with thick, rubberized soles during sports activities. These will provide you with the proper foot protection.

Wear heels with a broad base for support.

## Perfect Shoe Fit

The ball of your foot should fit comfortably in the widest part of the shoe.

You should have enough depth so that your toes don't rub the tops.

Stand up with the shoes on and make sure you have a half inch (about the width of your finger) between your longest toe and the front of the shoe.

Walk around in the shoes and make sure you don't experience any rubbing or slipping.

# No Socks Day Social Media Graphic

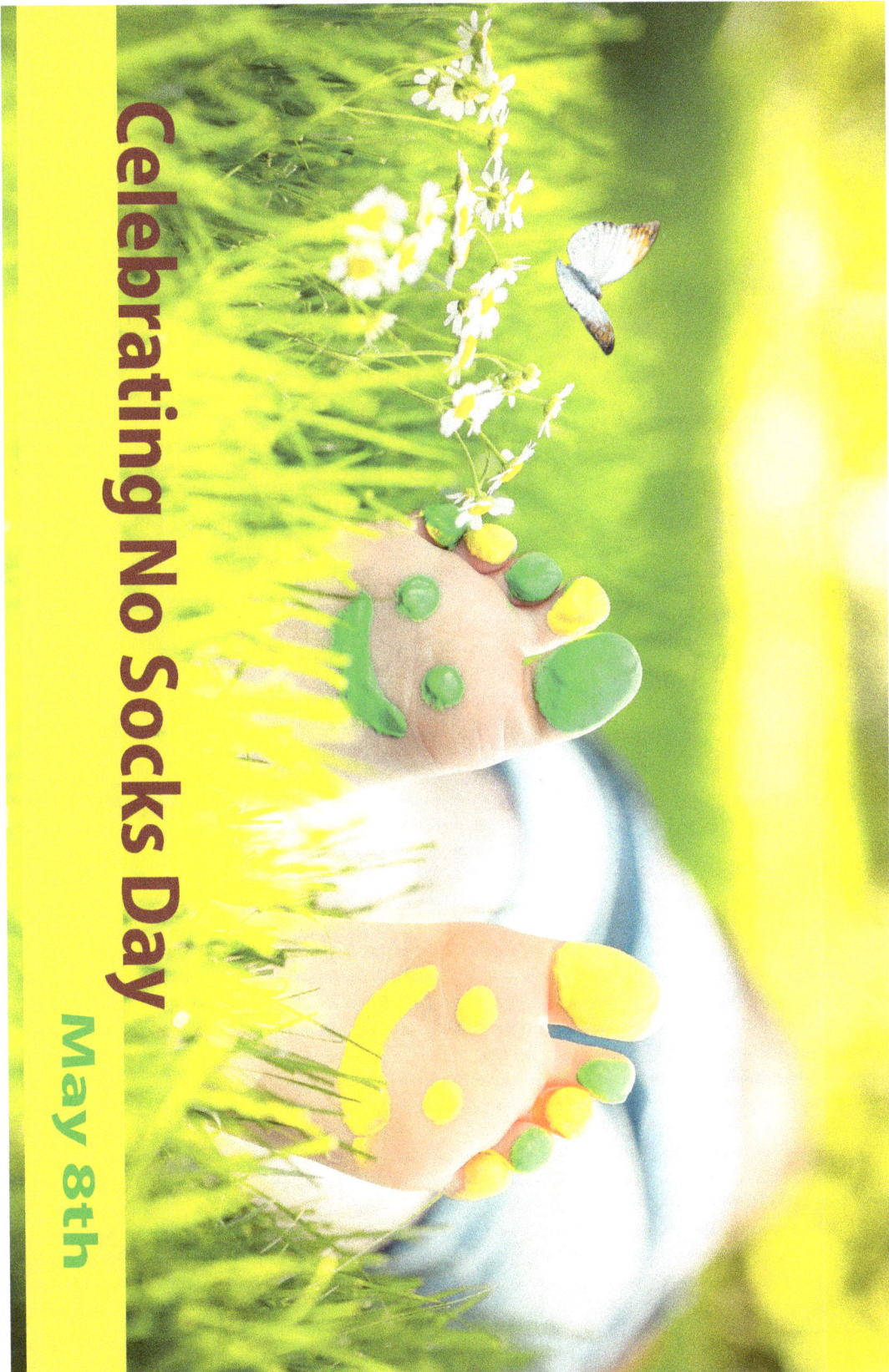

Celebrating No Socks Day

May 8th

# No Socks Day Clothing Drive Flyer

No Socks Day Drive
May 8th

Actions speak louder than words!
## GIVE TODAY

Accepted items:

Support the in-need children in our community.
[your text here]

Drop off Location:

SPONSORED BY:

# Friday the Thirteenth Facts

How often does Friday 13th occur?

> Every year will have at least one Friday the 13th, and the most it can ever have is three.

> Consecutive Friday the 13ths can occur in February and March provided it's not a leap year.

> The longest one can go without seeing a Friday the 13th is 14 months, after which there's no way of avoiding it.

> For a month to have a Friday the 13th it has to start on a Sunday. Count it out on your fingers like we just did — it's a fact.

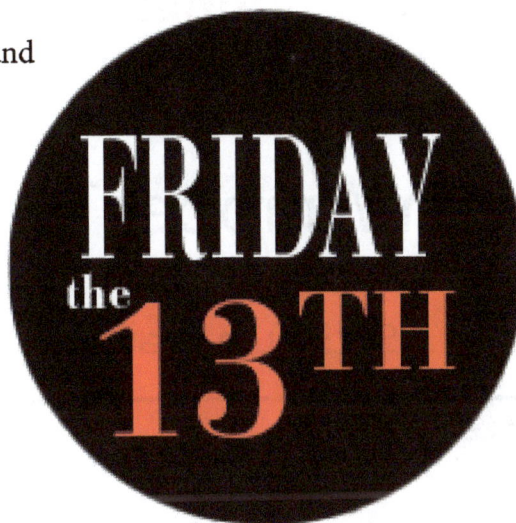

How many are there in 2022?

> Friday, May holds the only Friday the 13th in 2022.

> In 2023, there will be two Friday the 13ths falling in January and October.

> Last year had only one Friday the 13ths in August.

> Why don't you check your diaries to see if anything unfortunate happened to you on either one of those days?

Where does it get its reputation from?

> Many believe the superstition started in the Middle Ages and is rooted in the crucifixion.

> After all, Jesus Christ was betrayed on a Friday and there were 13 people at the Last Supper.

> Some also believe the day found its origins in 1307 when King Philip IV of France tortured and burned alive hundreds of Templar Knights.

Fear of Friday the 13th even has its own name.

> Friggatriskaidekaphobia. Frigga is the Norse goddess after which Friday is named, while triskaidekaphobia means a fear of the number thirteen.

> And there are plenty of things that have happened on this date to make you think it is indeed cursed — not least the fact that Fidel Castro and Margaret Thatcher were both born on one.

# National Candy Month Gum & Mini-Candy Wrappers Templates

## Gum Wrapper Templates

### Stick Gum Wrapper

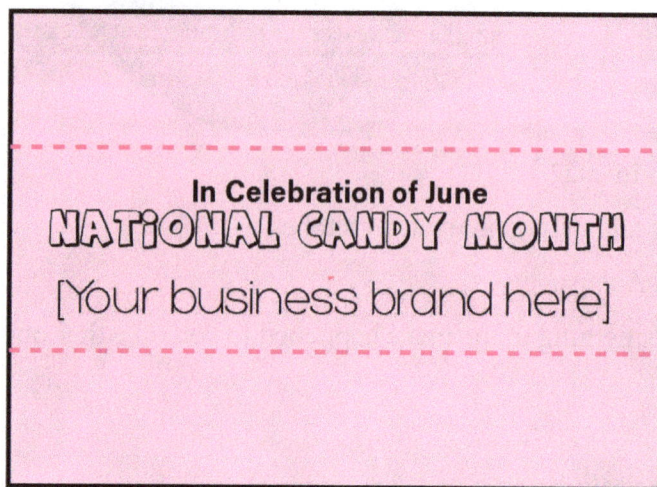

In Celebration of June
**NATIONAL CANDY MONTH**
[Your business brand here]

### Square Gum Wrapper

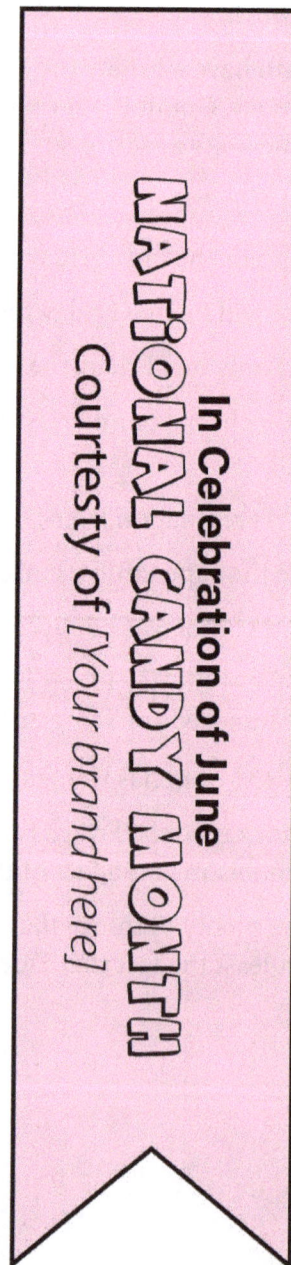

NATIONAL CANDY MONTH

In Celebration of June
NATIONAL CANDY MONTH
Courtesty of [Your brand here]

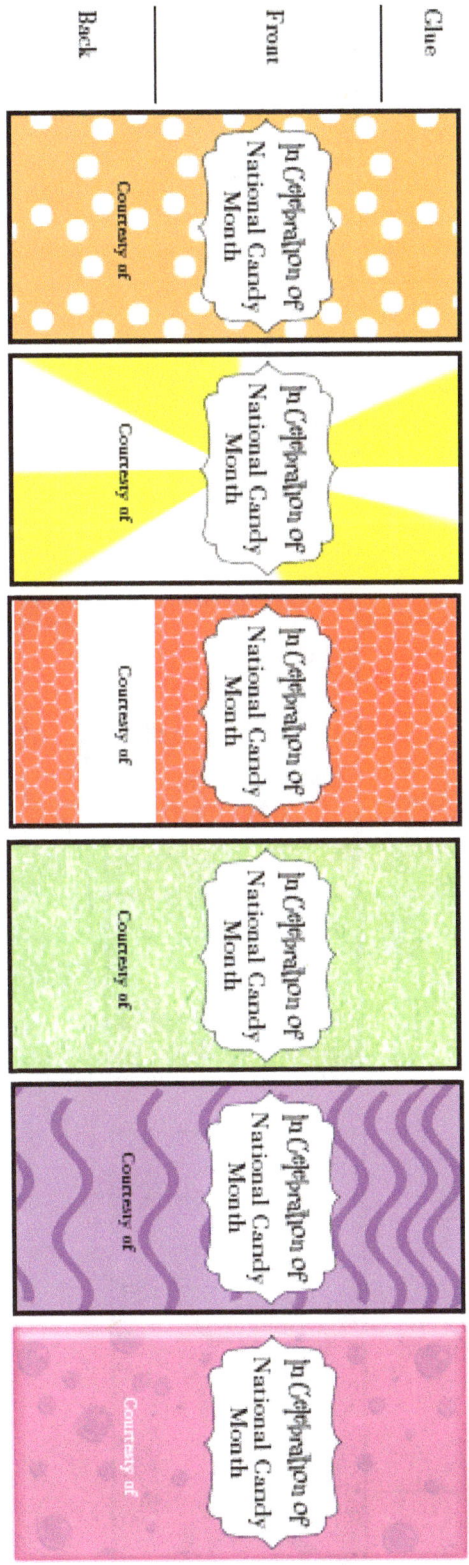

Hershey Mini Wrappers
Template by DocUmeantDesigns.com
Print Fit to Page Landscape

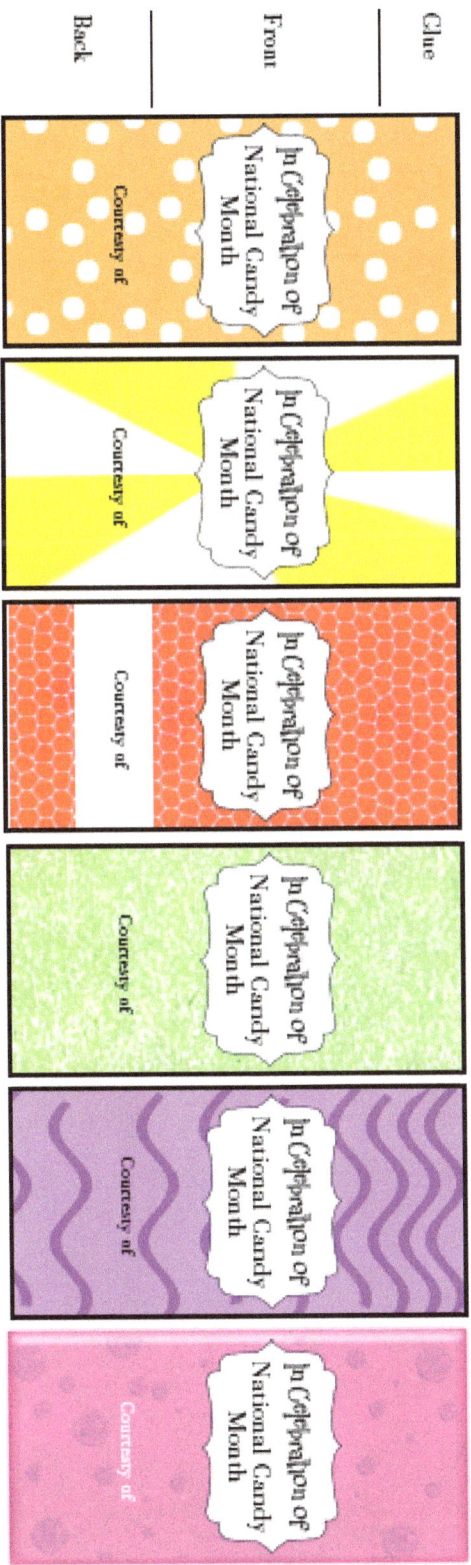

Glue | Front | Back

In Celebration of National Candy Month — Courtesy of

(repeated for each colored wrapper: orange polka dot, yellow, orange honeycomb, green, purple wavy, pink)

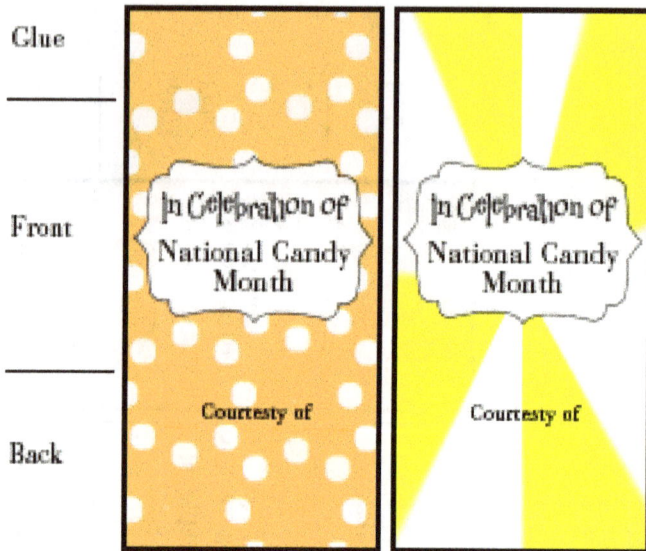

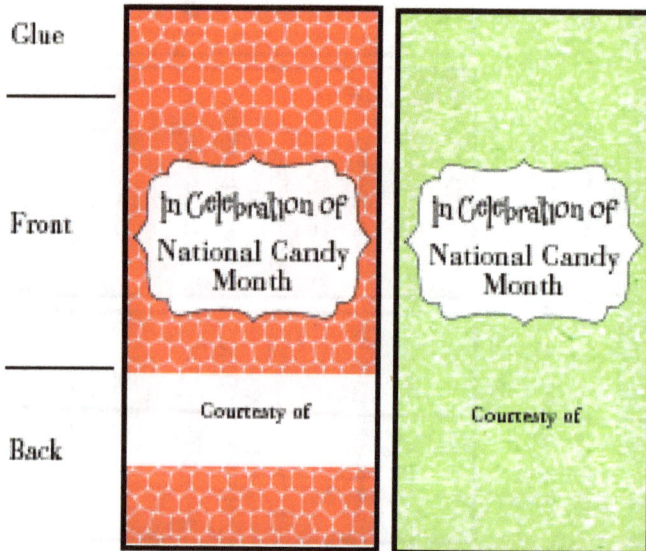

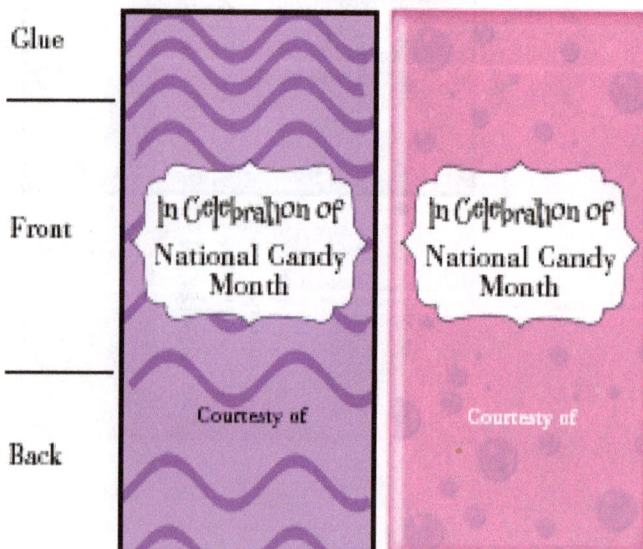

# Hawaiian Flying Saucer Recipe

Courtesy of Keeping it Relle

## Ingredients

Cooking oil of choice
1 small round onion, diced
1/2 green bell pepper, diced
3 cloves garlic, minced
1 pound ground beef
1/2 teaspoon salt
1/2 teaspoon pepper
1 cup ketchup
1/4 cup beef broth
2 tablespoons brown sugar
2 teaspoons Dijon or regular mustard
2 teaspoons Worcestershire sauce
1/2 cup corn
16 slices of bread, square or round
4 tablespoons butter
Cheese, shredded

## Directions

Add about a tablespoon of cooking oil to a large pan set over medium high heat. Add onion and bell pepper. Cook until onions just become translucent. Then add in garlic and cook until fragrant.

Next add ground beef, salt, and pepper. Cook until beef is no longer pink. IMPORTANT: Drain excess oil and return to the heat.

Then add ketchup, beef broth, brown sugar, mustard, and Worcestershire sauce. Mix until well combined, bring to a boil, then reduce heat to a simmer. Add corn. Cover and allow to simmer for 10–15 minutes stirring occasionally.

Remove from heat and set aside.

Now for the assembly. Lay a slice of bread down. Add shredded cheese and a few tablespoons of the beef mixture. Top with another slice of bread. Trim off the crust and press the edges of the sandwich together to seal it.

Add about a teaspoon of butter to a pan set over medium high heat. Place the sandwich in the pan and fry for a minute or two or until golden brown. Flip and repeat on the other side, adding more butter to the pan as needed.

Remove from heat and allow to cool slightly. ENJOY!

## Global Tiger Day Social Media Graphic

# Hidden Whale Graphic

# Spiderman Facts

Spiderman was created by Stan Lee and Steve Ditko for Marvel Comics.

Spiderman first appeared in the comic Amazing Fantasy #15 in August 1962.

Spiderman's alter ego is Peter Parker.

Spiderman's origin: while attending an exhibit on radioactivity, a spider descends from the ceiling between bands of radioactive ray beams and bites Peter's wrist.

Spiderman's adult supervisor was his Uncle Ben.

Spiderman's girlfriend is Mary Jane.

Before Spiderman became a superhero, he was a TV wrestler.

First actor who portrayed Spiderman was Nicholas Hammond.

## Spiderman Movies

Spiderman (2002)

Spiderman 2 (2004)

Spiderman 3 (2007)

The Amazing Spiderman (2012)

Spiderman Homecoming (2017)

Spiderman Far from Home (2019)

Spiderman Into the Spider-Verse

## Spiderman Villains[3]

As with Spider-Man, most of his villains' powers originate from scientific accidents or the misuse of technology. They can be classified into multiple categories, such as animal-themed villains (Doctor Octopus, Vulture, Lizard, Rhino, Scorpion, Jackal, Beetle, Kangaroo, Tarantula, and Puma), those with powers over the elements (Sandman, Electro, Molten Man, and Hydro-Man), horror-themed villains (the Green Goblin, the Hobgoblin, Morbius, Morlun, and the Symbiotes), crime lords (the Kingpin, Tombstone, Hammerhead, Silvermane, and Mister Negative), inventors (the Tinkerer, Spencer Smythe, and Alistair Smythe), and masters of trickery and illusion (the Chameleon and Mysterio). There are, however, numerous villains that don't fit into any specific category, such as Kraven the Hunter, the Shocker, and Mephisto, the latter of whom originated as a Silver Surfer villain. The villains oftentimes form teams such as the Sinister Six to oppose the web-slinger.

---

3      https://en.wikipedia.org/wiki/List_of_Spider-Man_enemies

www.coloring-painting-pages.com

Spider-Man is notable for having numerous villains that redeemed themselves and became antiheroes, such as Black Cat, the Prowler, Morbius, Kraven, and Silver Sable. Also, unlike most superheroes, Spider-Man doesn't have one particular archenemy, but rather three: the Norman Osborn version of the Green Goblin, Doctor Octopus, and the Eddie Brock version of Venom, the latter two of whom have been similarly redeemed and depicted as antiheroes.

# Charity Fundraising Drive

Courtesy of GoFundMe.com

Is there a cause that inspires you to support? Whether you're passionate about [fighting government corruption,] helping refugees, funding cancer research, or fighting poverty and hunger abroad, chances are there's a charity committed to that cause.

While not everyone can afford to give money to their favorite nonprofit, there are still ways to raise money for charity through different fundraising strategies. This charity fundraising guide offers tips on charitable giving so you can support charities that mean the most to you, regardless of your financial situation.

## Crowdfunding for a Good Cause

Traditional fundraising fosters relationship-building, while online fundraising makes it effortless to spread the word about your cause and reach people around the globe. Some of the most successful charity fundraisers use a combination of online and offline fundraising.

Crowdfunding allows you to support a charity close to your heart and has become an essential fundraising tool for individuals and small groups. It provides a simple, efficient way to accept donations from anyone. Many also turn to crowdfunding to pay for the cost of throwing a fundraising event.

## Five Strategies for Charity Crowdfunding Success

If you're searching for ways to take your online fundraiser to the next level, this guide can help. From grassroots volunteering to social media competitions, below we share charity fundraising ideas for any cause that can help you increase donations and raise money for charity.

## How to Raise Money for Charities

### 1. Talk to the nonprofit you're raising funds for

While people can absolutely raise money for nonprofit organizations without contacting them, it's best to reach out before getting started. This will help you follow any specific fundraising rules outlined by the charity since some nonprofits are strict about sources for charity funding. It will also ensure that you're fundraising for the correct nonprofit — a single nonprofit can have dozens of individual chapters, each with a unique tax number.

**When you contact the nonprofit you're helping, be sure to:**

- Ask if they have any upcoming events or promotions you could be a part of with other supporters

- Ask for any fundraising tips they might be able to share

- Ask if they have any swag you'd be able to use to promote your cause, such as keychains, bumper stickers, and pens.

## 2. Host your own fundraising event

From happy hours to amateur art exhibits, there's no shortage of fundraising event ideas. You can turn almost any event into an opportunity to raise money for a good cause — it just requires a bit of planning and ingenuity.

Fundraising events are a fantastic opportunity to build relationships with your community. The more your volunteers and supporters enjoy what they're doing, the more likely they are to do more of it — supporting your cause in the process.

### Keep these tips in mind when planning your fundraising event:

- To avoid stress and burnout, round up others who share a passion for your cause and ask them if they'd be interested in helping you out.

- It costs a bit of money upfront to host any kind of event, but budget event planning is still possible. Try asking local businesses to donate food and other needed items, or ask a restaurant or other business to host the event in exchange for the business you'll bring in.

- Send out event invitations through social media sites and encourage friends to bring along others. Using social media to promote your fundraiser can drum up support for your cause and encourage others to get involved.

- Read our blog posts about raising money with a charity walk and charity event ideas to help drive donations for more inspiration.

## 3. Get a little help from your friends

When you're fundraising, you'll often have supporters ask how they can help beyond making donations. The perfect reply? Ask them to volunteer their time.

If a volunteer is a fantastic baker, ask him or her to bake items you can sell, perhaps at a lunch or dinner event. Can an artist donate art you can sell at a gallery event? If you're raising money for a sports team, can the coach and players host an afternoon sports camp as a fundraiser? There are endless ways for volunteers to use their skills to bring in money for your charity.

Another way people can contribute is by sharing fundraising responsibilities. Our team fundraising feature makes it simple for multiple people to chip in and manage the fundraiser, whether that means thanking donors or writing updates.

For more information on team fundraising, see our blog post Fundraising for Teams: Tips for a Successful Fundraiser.

## 4. Empower others to do their own outreach

You can increase your fundraiser's reach exponentially by asking friends and family to share your cause with their contacts. Try using one of these email templates to reach your goal faster and make it as effortless as possible for others to ask for support.

Another approach is to craft the perfect public Facebook post about your fundraiser, then tag a few contacts and ask them to share the post. Pairing this approach with a compelling video is a great way to get people to stop scrolling and pay attention to your message.

**5. Sharpen your strategizing skills**

We want to help you reach your fundraising goals, and we offer fundraising tips on our blog to make it easy. If you're eager to learn more about how to raise money for charity, here are a few of our favorite posts:

- Charity Fundraising Tips for Any Cause
- Online Fundraising Without Social Media: 42 Ways to Share Offline
- 25 Best Charities to Donate to in the US (2019)
- Charity Crowdfunding Guide: How To Support Your Favorite Cause
- Top Charity Fundraising Sites to Make Giving Easier

## Support your favorite charity today

Nonprofits do an incredible amount of good, but they also need help to continue their mission. GoFundMe makes charity fundraising easy, and our fundraising platform allows you to keep more of your donations. Check out honest testimonials from users on the GoFundMe reviews page.

We hope this charity fundraising guide has helped you understand how to raise funds for charity and rally your community around your cause. To make an even bigger impact, start a fundraiser for your favorite nonprofit today.

# Play-Doh Recipe

Courtesy of Instructables.com

## Cooked

### Ingredients

2 cups flour
2 cups warm water
1 cup salt
2 Tablespoons vegetable oil
1 Tablespoon cream of tartar (optional for improved elasticity)
Food coloring (liquid, powder, or unsweetened Kool-Aid or similar drink mix)
Scented oils

### Directions

Mix all of the ingredients together and stir over low heat. The dough will begin to thicken until it resembles mashed potatoes.

IMPORTANT NOTE: if your playdough is still sticky, you simply need to cook it longer!

When the dough pulls away from the sides and clumps in the center, as shown below, remove the pan from heat and allow the dough to cool enough to handle.

Turn the dough out onto a clean counter or silicone mat and knead vigorously until it becomes silky-smooth. Divide the dough into balls for coloring.

Make a divot in the center of the ball, and drop some food coloring in. (If you use Kool-Aid or similar unsweetened drink mix for color, test on a small ball first- it won't go as far as the "real" food coloring.)

Fold the dough over, working the food color through the body of the playdough, trying to keep the raw dye away from your hands and the counter. You could use gloves, a big Ziplock bag, or plastic wrap at this stage to keep your hands clean — only the concentrated dye will color your skin, so as soon as it's worked in bare hands are fine.

Work the dye through, adding more as necessary to achieve your chosen color.

## Uncooked

(best for use when children are involved)

### Ingredients

1/2 cup salt
1/2 cup water
1 cup flour
Food dye (any color, be creative!)
Newspaper to cover the surface you're working on

## Directions

Measure out 1 cup of four and pour it into the bowl.

Then, measure out 1/2 cup of salt, and add that to the bowl, too.

Lastly, fill the measuring cup with 1/2 cup of water and pour it into the mixing bowl.

Use a spoon to mix up the ingredients. Mix it until it's mushy and it's neither watery nor flour-y.

Add a few drops of food dye to the mush, then pick it up and start kneading it. This is easy, just play around with it. If desired, add more food dye to improve color. You're finished!

If it's a little sticky, knead a tiny bit of flour into it. Use your imagination! You can make whatever you'd like!

When you're done, store your playdough in an air-tight container.

- If it begins to dry out, you can knead a bit of water in again to soften the dough back to usability. Once it's dried past a certain point, however, you'll just have to start over; thankfully, it's not terribly difficult.

- If it gets soggy, you can re-heat it to drive off the extra water the dough absorbed overnight. This is usually the result of high humidity but is fixable!

You can also bake it in the oven to make hard dough figures and ornaments, then paint or otherwise decorate the surface.

# Remote Employee Appreciation Day Social Media Graphic

# Poetry Facts

## Basics

Poetry's alias is Verse.

Poetry and Prose are not synonymous.

Types of poetry: Epic, Limerick, Riddles, Shapes, Sonnets, and Haiku.

In poetry, a block of lines is called a stanza.

The rhythm of a poem is called the meter.

A line with ten syllables is called a pentameter.

Poems that don't rhyme are called blank verse.

Poems with no meter (rhythm) is called free verse.

A limerick has five lines that rhyme. The first, second, and fifth rhyme with each other and the remaining third and fourth rhyme with each other.

Riddle poems don't have to rhyme.

Shape poems are poems where the lines of the poem are shaped into the main topic of the poem. An example of a shape poem is a poem about the sun in the shape of the spokes of the sun.

Sonnets have 14 lines and each stanza contains four lines with every other line rhyming. This is called a quatrain. The last two lines are called a couplet.

One of the most popular forms of writing short poems is the haiku. Originating from Japan, the haiku has only seventeen syllables. There are three lines containing five, seven, and again five syllables.

## History

Originally poetry was recited.

The oldest known epic poem is about 4,000 years old and is titled, Epic of Gilgamesh originating from Babylon.

The word "poetry" is from the Greek term poiesis, which means "making."

'Metrophobia' is the name for a fear of poetry.

'Metromania' denotes the compulsion to write poetry.

## Poets

The inventor of the limerick verse was the English poet, Edward Lear.

William Shakespeare wrote 154 sonnets.

The three best-selling poets in the world are Shakespeare, Lao-Tzu, and Khalil Gibran.

The shortest poem ever written was penned by George MacDonald and consisted of only two words, "Come Home."

The longest poem ever written is an Indian epic poem titled Mahabharata which has around 1.8 million words.

Seventeenth-century poet Sir John Suckling invented the card game cribbage.

German poet Gottlob Burmann so despised the letter R that he avoided using it in his poetry—and in everyday conversation.

The epitaph on Emily Dickinson's grave composed by the poet herself, consist of two words: 'called back'.

# Musical Games

## Name That Tune

Play, sing, or hum a tune and have the participants identify the song title. Extra credit if they can also name the band or signer who performed it.

Famous Singer Recognition

Similar to Name That Tune only use photos of the singers.

## Musical Charades

Similar to Name That Tune, have your players guess song titles by acting out the song or some of the words to the tune. Divide your participants into two or more teams. To keep the game short, you can use a timer. Can they do it before time expires?

For each song your team gets right, you advance on the board. The team that knows its music will get to the final square and win.

Suggested categories for this musical game are suited to various ages and musical preferences (Broadway musicals, television, movies, oldies, contemporary, folk, and family favorites). Recommended for players 18 years old and older.

## Who Sang This Tune?

Sing or hum the first few bars of their song. Have the players identify who the singer or band who made the song famous first.

## Musical Terms

Show flashcards with musical symbols on them and have the participants correctly name the term associated with it.

## Musical Chairs

This one needs no explanation. *wink*

## Telephone Tune

Create two teams and have the leader hum a tune into the first player's ear, who then passes it along to the next player, etc. The first team to correctly pass the tune along wins.

# Fill Our Staplers Day Social Media Graphic

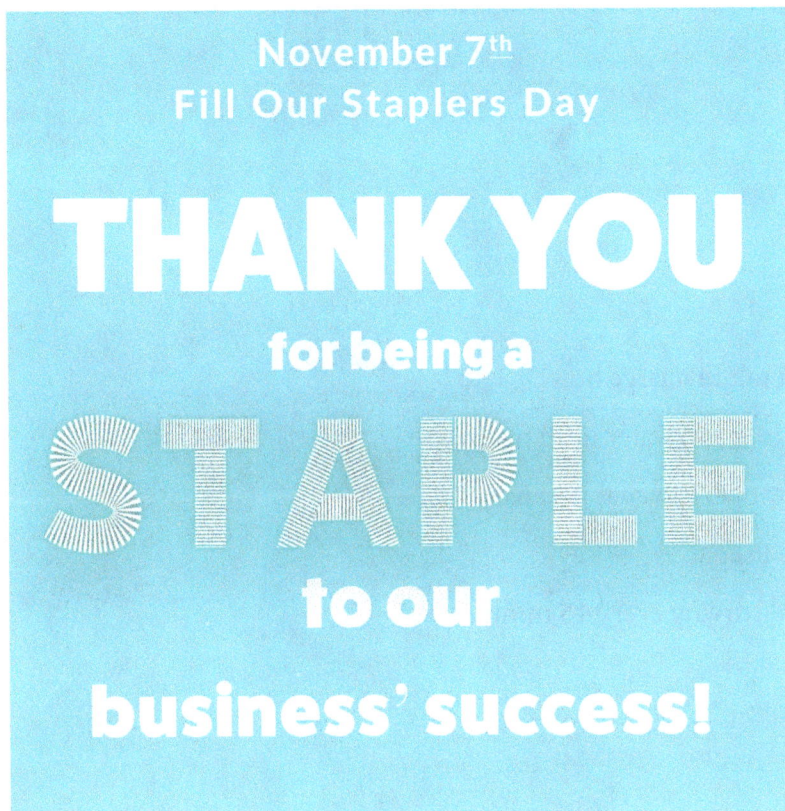

November 7th
Fill Our Staplers Day

**THANK YOU**
for being a
STAPLE
to our
business' success!

# Ginger's Favorite Recipes

## Candied Pecans

### Ingredients
1 cup sugar
1 teaspoon ground cinnamon
1 egg white
1 Tablespoon water
1 pound pecan halves

### Directions

Step 1: Combine sugar, cinnamon, and salt in a large bowl.

Step 2: In a medium bowl whisk egg white and water until frothy.

Step 3: Add pecan halves to egg white mixture to coat pecans.

Step 4: Pour pecans into sugar mixture to coat.

Step 5: Bake in 250-degree oven 1 hour, stirring every 15 minutes.

Store in airtight container.

## Cream Cheese Appetizer

### Ingredients
Cream Cheese
Mango Chutney
Bacon pieces
Pecan chips

### Directions
Layer all ingredients in the order given. Chill until ready to serve. Serve with fruit or butter crackers.

## Sweet Pumpkin Dip

### Ingredients
4 cups confectioners' sugar, sifted
2 8-ounce packages of cream cheese
1 30-ounce can pumpkin pie filling
2 teaspoons ground cinnamon
1 teaspoon ground Ginger

### Directions
In a large mixing bowl, combine sugar and cream cheese, beating until well blended. Beat in remaining ingredients. Store in an airtight container in the refrigerator.

Serve with Gingersnaps

# Paradise Island Salad with Coconut Mango Dressing

## Ingredients

**Dressing**

1 cup mayonnaise

8 – ounces sour cream

2 Tablespoons lime juice

1 cup mango chutney

15-ounce can Coco Lopez Cream of Coconut (comes in a can, like evaporated milk)

## Directions

In a medium bowl add all ingredients. Stir with a spoon until well blended. Set aside.

**Salad**

Butter lettuce, or baby greens, or Riviera Salad mix, etc.

Hearts of palm

Artichoke hearts

Mandarin Oranges

Strawberries

Walnuts

Pineapple, chunked

Coconut, flaked

On a platter place a bed of baby green or butter lettuce, etc.  Top with the remaining ingredients in order. Top with dressing just prior to serving.

# German Apple Pancake

## Ingredients

2 tablespoons butter

4 tablespoons sugar

3/4 teaspoon cinnamon

1 large tart apple, cored and sliced thinly

4 eggs

2/3 cup milk

1/3 cup flour

1/4 teaspoon salt

1 teaspoon vanilla (optional)

## Directions

Melt butter in 10-inch frying pan with oven proof handle (a well-seasoned cast iron skillet works great). Combine 3 tablespoons sugar with cinnamon and sprinkle evenly over butter. Arrange apple slices over sugar mixture in pan.

Cook over medium heat 3 – 4 min. Cool slightly.

Meanwhile, beat together eggs, milk, salt, flour, vanilla and 1 tablespoon remaining sugar. Pour gently over apple slices.

Bake at 400 degrees until golden brown and sides are puffy, approximately 15 – 20 minutes.

Serve immediately with maple syrup.

Serves 2

*If you like you can add an extra tablespoon of sugar to the sugar cinnamon mixture for a sweeter pancake.

## Malinda's Mac & Cheese Bake

### Ingredients
2 boxes macaroni & cheese (dry cheese mix)
1 stick butter (1/2 cup)
1 can carnation evaporated milk
1 package mild cheddar cheese
1 can cheddar cheese soup
3 – 4 eggs

### Directions
Boil dry macaroni according to package directions. Strain & pour into 9x11-inch baking dish.  Add chucks of butter and chucks on cheddar cheese while macaroni is still hot.  Add dry mix cheddar cheese, evaporated milk, chunks of cheddar cheese.  Mix well and add cheese soup.  Add beaten eggs. Mix all well.

Top with slices of cheddar cheese and bake in 350-degree oven for 1-hour or until cheese browns.

## Salmon Patties

### Ingredients
1 6-ounce can skinless, boneless salmon, drained
1/4 cup dry bread crumbs
1/4 cup dry bread crumbs (I use Parmesan bread crumbs)
1/4 cup finely chopped onions
2 Tablespoons mayonnaise or salad dressing
1 egg, beaten
1 teaspoon lemon juice
1 teaspoon parsley flakes
1/8 teaspoon garlic salt

---

Olive oil

### Directions
Step 1: In a medium bowl combine all ingredients except olive oil. Mix well.

Step 2: Shape into four patties. (Note: Mix will be moist.)

Step 3: In a frying pan with just a tiny bit of olive oil grill on both sides until brown.

Can be served on hamburger buns with your favorite sauce or served without the bun. I prefer to not use the buns.

## Alpermagronen

I discovered this yummy recipe while visiting in Switzerland.

### Ingredients
Tube Pasta
Potatoes
Onions
Parmesan Cheese
Cream

### Directions
Lots of chopped onion fried in olive oil until brown and crispy.

Boil chopped potatoes in saltwater, like potato salad.

Cook pasta as directed.

Pour all cooked ingredients into saucepan and mix with grated Parmesan cheese and cream.

Pat fried onions on top.

Serve with grated Parmesan cheese.

## Baked Parmesan Crusted Salmon

Baked Parmesan Crusted Salmon is a simple yet thoroughly impressive and satisfying seafood main dish! It's finishes with buttery, flaky salmon fillets coated in a golden-brown panko, Parmesan, and herb crust. Easy enough for a weeknight yet fitting enough for a holiday!

### Ingredients
4 skinless salmon fillets
3/4 cup panko bread crumbs
3/4 cup finely shredded Parmesan
2 1/2 Tablespoon chopped fresh parsley
3/4 teaspoon garlic powder
Salt and freshly ground black pepper, to taste
1 Tablespoon olive oil
1 large egg 4 lemon slices

### Directions
Preheat oven to 425 degrees. Spray an oven safe wire cooling rack with non-stick cooking spray and set over a rimmed 18 by 13-inch baking sheet.

In a shallow dish toss together panko, Parmesan, parsley, garlic powder, salt, and pepper. Drizzle in olive oil and toss well to evenly coat mixture.

In a separate shallow dish beat the egg until yolk and white are well blended.

Working with one piece of salmon at a time dredge each side in egg, then transfer to panko mixture and coat and press both sides of salmon in panko mixture (also sprinkle panko mixture over top and press to help stick).

Transfer to prepared wire rack on baking sheet. Repeat process with remaining 3 portions If you have extra breading sprinkle over fillets and gently press down to and even layer so they brown evenly.

Bake in preheated oven until salmon is barely cooked through, about 10–15 minutes (bake time will vary based on thickness of salmon).

Serve with lemon slices for spritzing over.

## Dump Cake

My baby sister, Valerie, gave me this recipe and told me that if I wanted to win a man's heart to make it. I did; it did. I also won his mother's heart as well.

### Ingredients
1 can of crushed pineapple
1 can of pie filling (I like to use peach or cherry)
Yellow cake mix
1/2 cup butter, melted
Pecans, optional

### Directions
In a 9 x 13-inch baking pan 'dump' all ingredients in the order provided.

Bake 350-degrees for 1 hour.

Serve with ice cream or whipped topping.

## No-bake Chocolate Oatmeal Cookies

### Ingredients
1⁄2 cup butter
1 1⁄2 cups white sugar
1⁄2 cup packed brown sugar
1⁄2 cup milk
4 tablespoons cocoa
1 pinch salt
1⁄2 cup creamy peanut butter
2 teaspoons vanilla
3 cups dry quick-cooking oats

## Directions

Add the first six ingredients into a 4-quart sauce pan.

Bring to a rolling boil and hold for 1 minute.

Remove from heat.

Add peanut butter into the hot mixture and stir until melted.

Add in vanilla. (Almond extract is good also, but I only use 1/2 teaspoon almond extract with 1 1/2 teaspoon vanilla extract).

Mix in the dry oats until they are completely coated.

Drop cookies by tablespoonfuls onto wax paper.

Let cool until set.

# Éclair Cake

## Ingredients
**Dough**
1 cup water
1 cup flour
1/2 cup butter (one stick)
4 eggs

**Pudding**

2 small packages white chocolate pudding mix
8-ounce package cream cheese, softened
3 ½ cups milk

## Directions

Mix water and butter in small saucepan and heat until butter melts. Stir in flour and cook until ball of dough forms. Cool 5-minutes and add 4 eggs one at a time.

Spread into 9x13-inch pan. Smooth with damp fingers. Bake 400-degree oven for 30 minutes. Cool.

Mix pudding incredients until firm. Add cool whip. Pour into shell and chill until firm. Top with drizzled chocolate sauce.

# Eye Facts

## General Facts

Your eyes start to develop two weeks after you are conceived.

Newborns don't produce tears. They make crying sounds, but the tears don't start flowing until they are about 4 – 13 weeks old.

Your eyeballs stay the same size from birth to death.

A fingerprint has 40 unique characteristics, but an iris has 256.

"Red eye" occurs in photos because light from the flash bounces off the back of the eye. The choroid is located behind the retina and is rich in blood vessels, which make it appear red on film.

The average blink lasts for about 1/10th of a second.

You blink about 12 times every minute.

Women blink nearly twice as much as men.

Some people are born with two differently colored eyes. This condition is heterochromia.

Even if no one in the past few generations of your family had blue or green eyes, these recessive traits can still appear in later generations.

Each of your eyes has a small blind spot in the back of the retina where the optic nerve enters. You don't notice the hole in your vision because your eyes work together to fill in each other's blind spot.

Out of all the muscles in your body, the muscles that control your eyes are the most active.

The entire length of all the eyelashes shed by a human in their life is over 98 feet with each eye lash having a life span of about 5 months.

80% of vision problems worldwide are avoidable or even curable.

Theodore Roosevelt is the only president who lost an eye while still in office.

The giant squid has the largest eye.

The most common injury caused by cosmetics is to the eye by a mascara wand.

## Donor Facts

More than 100,000 Americans need eye, tissue, or organ donations.

Worldwide, a shortage of corneas for transplant leaves too many people waiting for the chance to see.

Age, cataracts, prior surgeries (including laser eye surgery), most cancers, and poor vision DO NOT necessarily prevent one from being a donor.

Donation must occur within hours of death.

Donation can occur at a hospital, in a hospice setting, and at a funeral home.

Donors are treated with dignity and respect.

While the cornea (the clear tissue in the front of the eye) is the only part of the eye regularly transplanted, the sclera (white of the eye) can also be used in some surgeries.

The entire eye can be used for research and education.

Becoming a donor is easy. All you need to do is decide to become a donor and then make it legal or at least known.

- Mark your license as "donor"
- Register on DonateLifeMN
- Register when applying for a hunting or fishing license
- Carry a donor card
- Put your donation wishes in a health care directive
- Tell your family

Eye donation continues during COVID-19.

Over 97% of all corneal transplant operations successfully restore the corneal recipient's vision!

Eye banks in the United States provided 84,297 corneas for transplant in 2017 and provided a further 28,000 corneas for use internationally.

Since 1961, more than 1,800,000 men, women, and children worldwide have had their sight restored through corneal transplantation.

It costs the donor family nothing to donate eyes, organs, or tissue.

# Give the Gift of Sight Month Infographic

Anyone can be an eye donor regardless of age, ethnicity, or medical history.

Eye donation gives sight to two blind persons as each is given one eye.

More than 100,000 Americans need eye, tissue, or organ donations.

Over 97% of all corneal transplant operations successfully restore the patient's vision!

Eye donation contines during COVID-19.

This means that cornea transplants are still accessible nationwide.

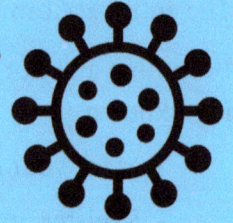

Additionally, cornea research about the impact of COVID-19 is in progress.

There is no cost to the donor family or recipient for the donation.

The entire eye can be used for research and education.

Becoming a donor is easy. All you need to do is decide to become a donor and then make it legal or at least known.

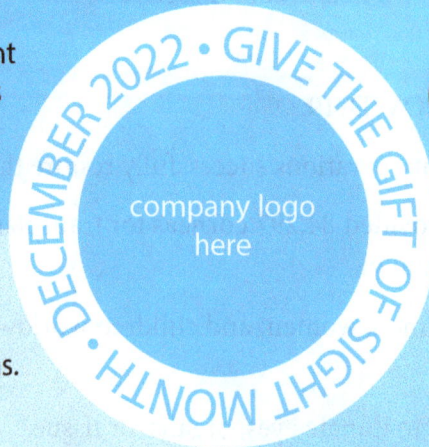

DECEMBER 2022 • GIVE THE GIFT OF SIGHT MONTH •

company logo here

# Kaleidoscope Day Event Flyer

## Kaleidoscope Day Webinar

### Discover How to Reach Your Goals in the New Year

Join us on Kaleidoscope Day to reflect on your business' potential
for a whole new spectrum of ideas!

Keynote speaker
photo

speaker

speaker

alternet
speaker photo
holder

Dec 11, 2022
Venue:
Time:

**RSVP Required.
Contact:**

# Appendix B: Social Media Image Size Guide

All dimensions given in pixels.

## FACEBOOK

Cover Photo: 820 x 310 (mobile 640 x 320)

Profile Image: 180 x 180 (smartphone 128 x 128)

Fan Page Cover Video 820 x 312

Shared Link: 484 x 252

Shared Square: 1200 will display at 470

Event Image: 1920 x 1080

Ad: 470 x 246 (computer); 560 x 292 (mobile); 254 x 113 (vertical)

Online Display Promotions: 470 x 470 (computer); 626 x 840 (mobile); 254 x 133 (horizontal)

## LINKEDIN

Profile Image: 400 x 400

Background Image: 1584 x 396

Shared Image: 529 x 320

Shared Image w/link: 520 x 272

## YOUTUBE

Channel Profile: 100 x 100

Channel Cover Photo: 2560 x 1440

Video Uploads: 1280 x 720

## INSTAGRAM

Profile Image: 110 x 110

Photo Thumbnail: 161 x 161

Photo Size: 1080 x 1080

Landscape: 1080 x 566

Portrait: 1080 x 1350

Online Display Promotions: 1080 (square will appear 640); 1080 x 566 (horizontal will appear 600 x 400)

## TWITTER

Header Photo: 1500 x 500

Profile Photo: 400 x 400 (displays at 200 x 200)

Timeline Photo: 1024 x 512

Twitter Cards: 800 x 418 pixels or 800 x 800

## PINTEREST

Profile Image: 280 x 280

Giraffe Pin: 600 x 1560

Pin Sizes: 600 x 750 (portrait); 600 (square); 600 x 900 (optimal); 600 x 1200 (infographic — only one part will appear, clicking will be complete)

## TUMBLER

Profile Image: 128 x 128

Image Posts: 500 x750

## GOOGLE+

Profile Image: 250 x 250

Cover Image: 1084 x 610

Shared Image: 530 wide

Shared Link Image: 530 wide

## ELLO

Banner Image: 1800 x 1300

Profile Image: 340 x 340

## SNAPCHAT

Geofilter Image: 1080 x 1920

# Chinese Social Media

## WECHAT

Profile Photo: 200 x 200

Article Preview Header: 900 x 500

Article Preview Thumbnail: 400 x 400 (displays at 200 x 200)

Article Inline Image: 400 wide x any height

## WEIBO

Cover Image: 920 x 300

Profile Picture: 200 x 200 (displays at 100 x 100)

Banner: 550 x 260

Instream: 120 x 120

Contest Preview: 288 x 288

Contest Picture: 640 x 640

Contest Poster: 570 wide

Prize Picture:200 x 200

# Appendix C: LINKS

## Link Checker
For Chrome: https://chrome.google.com/webstore/detail/check-my-links/ojkcdipcgfaekbeaelaapa-kgnjflfglf?hl=en-GB (I know this is out of alpha order, but a good link deserves top billing, don't you think? ;)

## Article Marketing Sites
http://goarticles.com/

http://internationalpractice.com/business/

http://thephantomwriters.com/index.php

http://www.articledashboard.com/

http://www.articlegarden.com/

http://www.articlesbase.com/

http://www.articleson.com/

http://www.sitepronews.com/

http://www.selfgrowth.com

http://marniemarcus.com/unplugged/facebook-ad-management/

http://www.isnare.com

http://www.ladypens.com/

http://www.promotionworld.com

http://www.writeandpublishyourbook.com/magazine/

https://contributor.yahoo.com/signup.shtml

http://www.ezinearticles.com

## Auto Responder Services
AWeber: www.aweber.com/

Constant Contact: https://www.constantcontact.com/

Robly: https://app.robly.com/invite?rc=f56a53fb2ad6910f3e83ebda

Your Mailing List Provider: www.yourmailinglistprovider.com/

## Books and Movies

#Next Level Manners: Business Etiquette for Millennials by Rachel Isgar Ph.D.: https://pleasepass-themanners.com/work/

The Baby Boomer/Millennial Divide: Making it work at work by Beverly Mahone: https://tinyurl.com/BBMD-BM

Complete Library of Entrepreneurial Wisdom by Ginger Marks: http://www.CLEWbook.com

Customer Service Skills for Success by Robert W Lucas: https://www.robertwlucas.com

Emotional Intelligence in Christ by Estella Chavous, Rich Cummins, Lauren E Miller, with Ken Voges https://emotionalintelligenceinchrist.com/

Presentational Skills for the Next Generation by Ginger Marks: https://www.DocUmeantPublishing.com

Emotional Intelligence Test Websites

Campbellsville University: https://online.campbellsville.edu/business/emotional-intelligence-test/

Greater Good Magazine: https://greatergood.berkeley.edu/quizzes/ei_quiz/

Institute of Health and Human Potential: https://www.ihhp.com/free-eq-quiz/

PSYMed: https://psymed.info/eq-test

Psychology Today: https://www.psychologytoday.com/us/tests/personality/emotional-intelligence-test

## Greeting Card Companies

123Greetings: http://www.123greetings.com

American Greetings: http://www.americangreetings.com/

Blue Mountain: www.bluemountain.com/

Cyberkisses: http://www.cyberkisses.com/

Day Springs: www.dayspring.com/ecards/

Evite: www.evite.com

Hallmark: https://www.hallmark.com/

Jacquie Lawson: www.jacquielawson.com/

Just Wink: https://www.justwink.com/

Operation Write Home: http://operationwritehome.org/

Punchbowl Greetings: http://www.punchbowl.com/invitations/preview/5400a4b424e4b36a3e000029/5400a56bbf947f655a000111

Send Out Cards: www.sendoutcards.com/

## Podcast Directories

Corante-Podcasting: http://podcasting.corante.com/ —Weblog with news and events related to podcasting.

Hipcast: http://www.hipcaStcom/ —Audio and video podcasting service. Includes news and on-line tour.

iTunes: https://www.apple.com/itunes/ —The iTunes Store puts thousands of free podcasts at your fingertips.

Lextext.com: How to Podcast RIAA Music Under License —http://blog.lextext.com/blog/_archives/2005/1/4/225172.html —Discussion of legal ways to podcast music. [Podcast is 5.3 MB in size]

The Liberated Syndication Network: http://www.libsyn.com/ —Full featured service tailored specifically for media Self-publishing and podcasting. Price is based on usage, changing monthly if needed.

NPR: http://www.npr.org/rss/podcast/podcast_directory.php —Over 50 public radio stations and producers are working with NPR to bring you podcasting.

Podcasting News: http://www.podcastingnews.com/ —Information relating to podcasting, a podcast directory, and a user forum.

SkypeCasters: http://www.henshall.com/blog/archives/001056.html —Introducing instructions for SkypeCasting, the solution for podcasters to create audio recordings from interviews and conference calls using Skype.

Skype Forums: https://answers.microsoft.com/en-us/skype/ —Recording a Skype Conversation–Discussion thread covering software, techniques, and legal tidbits.

Wikipedia: Podcast –http://en.wikipedia.org/wiki/Podcast —Encyclopedia entry covering basics of the topic.

## Promotional Product Supply Companies

4imprint: https://www.4imprint.com —for free samples

Build a Sign: http://www.buildasign.com/

CafePress: www.cafepress.com/

Crown Awards: https://www.crownawards.com/

iPrint: https://www.iprint.com/estore/

Judie Glenn Inc: www.judieglenninc.com —ask for Tracey Arehart

Northwest Territorial Mint: http://custom.nwtmint.com/

Overnight Prints: http://www.overnightprints.com/

PC/Nametag®: http://www.pcnametag.com/

Promotional Products: www.promotionalproducts.org/ —Get free quotes from multiple vendors

Staples: www.StaplesPromotionalProducts.com

VistaPrint: www.Vistaprint.com

World Class Medals: http://www.worldclassmedals.com/

Zazzle: http://www.zazzle.com/custom/buttons

## Quote Sources

Bartleby: http://www.bartleby.com/

Brainy Quote: http://www.brainyquote.com/quotes/keywords/resources.html

Leadership Now: http://www.leadershipnow.com/quotes.html

Quote Garden: http://www.quotegarden.com/index.html

Quoteland: http://www.quoteland.com/

The Quotations Page: http://www.quotationspage.com/

Think Exit: http://thinkexist.com/quotes/american_proverb/

Woopidoo!: http://www.woopidoo.com/

## Stock Photos

Tiny Eye: http://www.tineye.com —Reverse image search

Adobe Stock: https://stock.adobe.com/

Alamy: http://www.alamy.com

Beinecke: http://beinecke.library.yale.edu/digitallibrary

Maps Download MrSid: http://memory.loc.gov/ammem/help/download_sid.html

Big Stock Photo: http://www.bigstockphoto.com

Bing: http://www.bing.com

Can Stock Photo: http://www.canstockphoto.com

CreStock: http://www.crestock.com

DepositPhotos: http://depositphotos.com

Digital Scriptorium: http://bancroft.berkeley.edu/digitalscriptorium —public domain

Dreamstime: https://www.dreamstime.com

EJ Photo: https://ejphoto.com/ —Nature photography

Flickr: https://www.flickr.com — Advanced Search (only search on commercial content etc.)

Foto Search: http://www.fotosearch.com

Free Digital Photos: http://www.freedigitalphotos.net

Free Photo: http://www.freefoto.com/index.jsp

Getty: http://www.gettyimages.com/

Google: http://www.images.google.com — Use Advanced Search for Usage Rights, labeled with commercial w/modifications

Icon Finder: http://www.iconfinder.com/illustrations

iStockPhoto: http://www.iStockPhoto.com

Jupiter: http://www.jupiterimages.com

Library of Congress: http://www.loc.gov/index.html — American Memory and Prints and Photographs sections

Morguefile: http://morguefile.com

PhotoSpin: https://www.photospin.com/Default.asp?

Pixabay: http://pixabay.com/

Pixadus: http://pixdaus.com

RGB Stock: https://www.rgbstock.com/ — more than 95,000 high quality free stock photos, graphics for illustrations, wallpapers, and backgrounds

Scriptorium: http://www.scriptorium.columbia.edu/ public domain

Shutterstock: http://www.shutterstock.com

Stockxchg (FreeImages): http://www.sxc.hu/

ThinkStock Photos: http://www.thinkstockphotos.com/

Top Left Pixel: http://wvs.topleftpixel.com

VectorStock: https://www.vectorstock.com/royalty-free-vectors

Visipix: http://www.visipix.com — lots of Japanese art

Visual Photos: http://www.visualphotos.com

Watercolor Textures: https://lostandtaken.com/downloads/category/paint/watercolor-texture/

WebStockPro: http://www.webstockpro.com/

Wikimedia Commons: http://commons.wikimedia.org/wiki/Main_Page —Check images via languages

Wikipedia: https://en.wikipedia.org/wiki/Wikipedia:Public_domain_image_resources

You Work for Them: https://www.youworkforthem.com

## Teleconference Companies

What is: www.business.com/directory/telecommunications/business_solutions/conferencing/

Buyer's Guide: www.buyerzone.com/telecom_services/telecon_services/buyers_guide5.html

Free Conference: www.freeconference.com/

Teleconference Live: http://teleconference.liveoffice.com

Teleconferencing Services: www.teleconferencingservices.net/

Yugma Desktop Sharing Software: http://vur.me/gmarks/Yugma/

Zoom: https://www.zoom.us

## Tools

Webp to Jpg, Tif, png Converter

https://www.freeconvert.com/webp-to-jpg

## Virtual Assistant Companies

A Clayton's Secretary (Kathie M Thomas): http://vadirectory.net/

Streamline Your Marketing (Crystal Pina): https://streamlineyourmarketing.com/

https://www.freeconvert.com/webp-to-jpg

## Webinar Services

Adobe Acrobat Connect Pro: http://tryit.adobe.com/us/connectpro/universalvoice/?sdid=DNOSU

BrainShark: http://brainshark.com/

Cisco WebEx: http://webex.com/

ClickMeeting: https://clickmeeting.com/

Elluminate: http://www.elluminate.com/Products/?id=3

Facebook Live: https://live.fb.com/

Freebinar: http://www.freebinar.com/

Free Conference Calling: http://www.freeconferencecalling.com/

Fuze: http://www.fuzemeeting.com/

GatherPlace: http://www.gatherplace.net/start/

Google+ Hangouts: https://plus.google.com/hangouts

GoToMeeting: https://www.gotomeeting.com/

GoToWebinar: http://www.gotomeeting.com/fec/webinar

IBM Lotus Unyte: https://www.unyte.net/

iLinc: http://www.ilinc.com/

Infinite Conference: http://www.infiniteconference.com/

InstantPresenter: http://www.instantpresenter.com/

Intercall: http://www.intercall.com/smb/

Mega Meeting: http://www.megameeting.com/professional.html

Nefsis: http://www.nefsis.com/

ReadyTalk: https://www.readytalk.com/

Saba Centra: http://saba.com/

SalesForce: https://www.salesforce.com/

StageToWeb: http://www.stagetoweb.com/livE-event–webcasting.html

Tokbox: http://tokbox.com/

Video Seminar Live: http://www.videoseminarlive.com/

Wix: http://www.wix.com/

Yugma: https://www.yugma.com/

Zoho: http://www.zoho.com/meeting/

# Appendix D: RESOURCES

Charity Fundraising: https://www.gofundme.com/c/blog/raise-money-charity

Clean-Up Your Computer Infographic: https://recoverit.wondershare.com/partition-tips/free-up-hard-drive-space-on-windows-10.html

Friday the 13th: https://metro.co.uk/2021/08/13/friday-the-13th-how-often-does-it-occur-15081713/

Keeping it Relle: https://keepingitrelle.com/hawaiian-style-flying-saucer-recipe/

LifeSource, Eye Donation: https://www.life-source.org/latest/five-facts-about-eye-donation/

Merriam-Webster's Great Big List of Beautiful and Useless Words, Vol. 3: https://www.merriam-webster.com/words-at-play/beautiful-useless-obscure-words-volume-3/

Memory Games: https://myallamericancare.com/blog/2020/02/26/top-6-fun-and-memory-games-for-seniors/

Play-Doh Recipe: https://www.instructables.com/How-to-Make-Playdough-Play-doh/

See's Candies: https://www.sees.com/

If you found this book interesting, helpful, motivational, fun, or any of the other numerous adjectives that have been used to describe this award-winning book, I would love to read your comments. Please let others know what a valuable asset you have found by leaving your review on your favorite book seller website.

---

If you would like to have a personal coaching session on how you can use this book to market your business send Ginger an email at ginger.marks@documeantdesigns.com and let her know. This valuable coaching service can be purchased for $295.00 per year and includes personal one-on-one coaching four times per year.

# Thank you!

# About the Author

Ginger is the owner of the Calomar, LLC which holds her DocUmeant family of companies. The various entities all work towards a common goal that just happens to be their tagline; "We Make YOU Look GOOD!" Her services include both publishing and digital design assistance. She is proud of the fact that she is able to give high quality, efficient service at a remarkably reasonable rate. It is for this reason she chose to list her publishing company in New York City while residing in Florida.

When Ginger decided to embark on a writing career it was of no surprise to her mother, who herself is a published author. Her love for the arts is what spurred her to hone her talents as a digital designer, offering services to business owners and authors alike.

DocUmeant.net offers editing and writing services; DocUmeantDesigns.com, as you would guess, focuses on designs ranging from websites to book covers and layouts to buttons and business stationery needs; while DocUmeantPublishing.com's focus was begun with the self-published author in mind. Now with ten years of experience in publishing she has built her success in the global community.

Ginger is a member of DesignFirms where she is a top-rated designer, SPANpro (Small Publishers Association of North America), IBPA (International Book Publishers Association), DBW (Digital Book World), and is on the board of FAPA as VP Communications (Florida Authors and Publishers Association).

Most recently, Ginger was awarded for her generous contribution to internet business while helping others achieve their goals in publishing and marketing. The Golden Mouse Award was presented to her by Women In e-Commerce on Oct 28, 2016. In 2012 she was awarded VIP membership to Covington's Who's Who and her publishing company, DocUmeant Publishing, was awarded the 2012 and 2016 New York Award in the Publishing Consultants and Services category by the U.S. Commerce Association (USCA). She recently won the 2015 and 2016 Clearwater, FL Design Firm Award and has won book cover design awards and is a multiple award winner for her *Weird and Wacky Holiday Marketing Guide* from FAPA.

In her spare time, she loves to do crafts of all sorts and sing. And yes, she is a little wacky at times too which keeps her fun and inspiring. Ginger lives in Florida where she works side-by-side with her husband, Philip, who is VP Editing for DocUmeant Publishing.

To contact Ginger whether for publish, design, or interviews you may reach her at ginger.marks@documeantdesigns.com or at 727-565-2130.

# Additional Works

by Ginger Marks

Visit DocUmeantPublishing for more information or to purchase her books.

https://www.DocUmeantPublishing.com

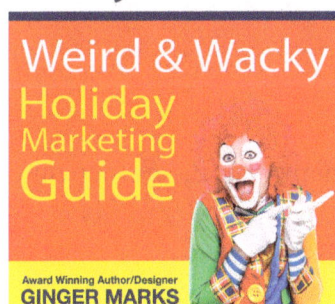

ISBN-13: 978-1937801779

The companion Playbook for the Annual *Weird and Wacky Holiday Marketing Guide* l will assist you in planning and tracking your holiday marketing success using the tools, tips, and resources found in the *Weird and Wacky Holiday Marketing Guide.*

- Easily plan and track your marketing
- Organized by month
- Room to write notes
- Track your success
- No expiration date! Start using any time.

Print: $12.97 Available at https://www.DocUmeantPublishing.com

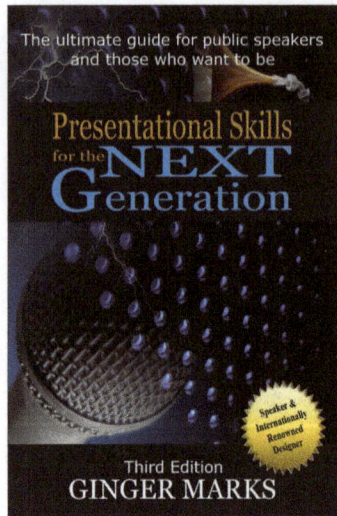

Print ISBN: 978-0-9788831-4-0

eBook ISBN: 978-0-9832122-7-0

Much has changed over the years in the public speaking arena. We have so many new and challenging tools at our disposal that we are no longer consigned to countless hours to travel from city to city to share our knowledge.

The internet has opened the doors to people from all places and races. At the click of a button, you can share your information in many forms of multi-media. With the availability of hosting online conferences and collaborations in both text-only and A/V environments, as are offered by Skype Conference™, Hot Conference™ and desktop sharing applications such as Yugma™, as well as teleconferences, the modes and means are so plentiful that more and more savvy business owners are venturing into the public speaking arena.

It is a well thought out, concise, instructional manual written in a manner that all can comprehend. Within the contents of this guide, you will learn the skills necessary to enable you to present your information in such a way that you will capture the attention and hearts of your eager audience.

Available in Print $14.95

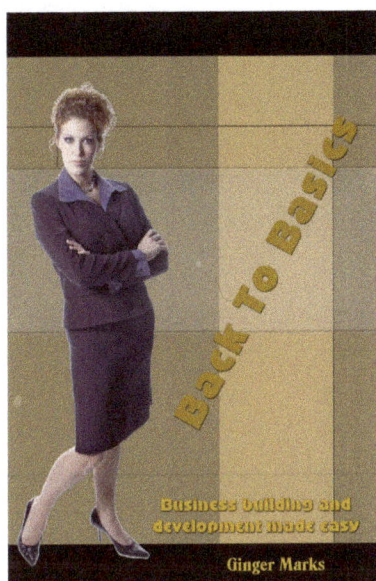

*Back to Basics* is a collection of articles designed to assist the new business owner to jump start their business or the seasoned profession to put the punch back into their chosen career. It begins with a two-part series on the Nuts and Bolts of Business Building and continues from there to the ever-important Marketing Basics. As marketing is an issue for each and every business owner no matter their business or circumstances this section is presented in three parts. This eBook comes in Kindle and PDF versions and at $2.99 it is a real bargain.

$2.99 eBook Edition

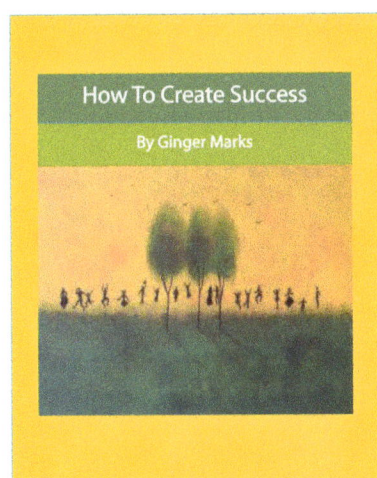

*How To Create Success* is the first eBook offering. Its bold colorful cover image entitled Jumping for Joy was designed by Amanda Tomasoa of Art by Amanda. The seven chapters contained within combine seven of the most highly rated articles written by Ginger at the time of publishing. One article Contagious Influence is currently the number one requested article and has been published in a magazine for writers titled 'Newbie News'. This is a free ebook and available for immediate download.

FREE: To download follow this link: http://www.gingermarksbooks.com/PDFs/HowToCreateSuccess.pdf.

SPECIAL REPORT

# How to Create Long Sales Copy Web Pages

**DocUmeant Designs.com**

In this report you will learn how to create an effective Long Sales Copy Web Page and why you might need one. As you read through this report if you come to the conclusion that a Long Sales Copy Web Page is the right tool for your business, I highly recommend you use the company or individual with the working knowledge and integrity to create the site you need to get your important message across to your target market.

If you haven't a clue how to decipher who your target market is then that it the best place to start. Without this knowledge, no matter how compelling your product or service message is, it will result in an ineffective campaign. This will end up costing valuable time and money. Although this is beyond the context of this Special Report there are a myriad of resources available to you today online to help you along the way. As well, there are coaches who specialize in this area of expertise. Feel free to contact me and I will be happy to point you in the right direction.

To reccive this FREE REPORT sign up for her monthly Words of Wisdom eZine at http://www.gingermarksbooks.com/.

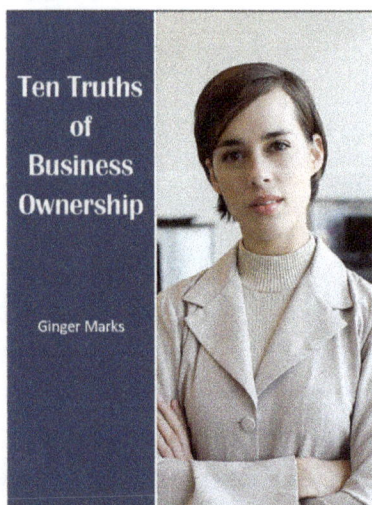

**Ten Truths of Business Ownership**

Ginger Marks

Discover the 10 truths every business owner should know. Knowing and applying these truths will aide you in achieving your dream of entrepreneurship.

To receive this eBook along with Ginger Marks' report *How to Create Long Sales Copy Web Pages* sign up for her monthly Words of Wisdom eZine here.

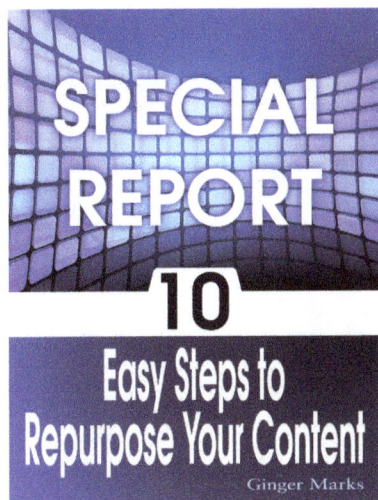

Get your copy of Ginger's Free Special Report: *10 Easy Steps to Re-purpose Your Content.*

This is the insider's view of how the *Complete Library of Entrepreneurial Wisdom* came about. With the information you will garner in this Special Report, you too can quickly and easily create your very own new money maker.

To download visit http://clewbook.com/

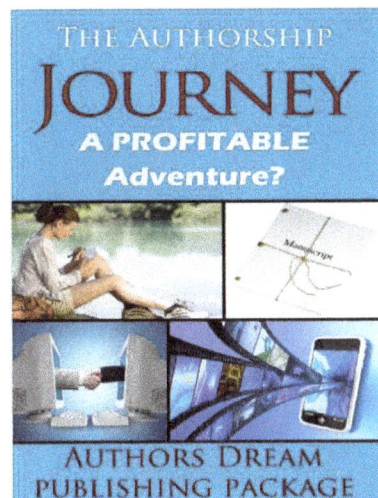

*The Journey to Authorship* is a road few travel. Find out how you too can traverse the challenges that lie ahead and come out on top. Advice from leading experts in the field.

Digital $0.99

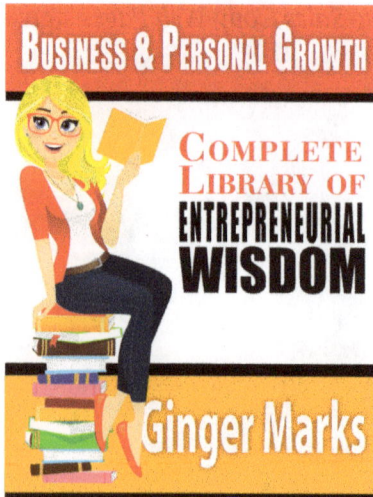

Hardcover ISBN: 978-1937801380

Paperback ISBN: 978-1494928292

*The Complete Library of Entrepreneurial Wisdom* covers business basics, including how to and how not to start your business; marketing; marketing design, which is a topic rarely covered; writing, which covers technical, practical, as well as, marketing aspects to writing; and life reflections, such as planning for emergencies and disasters — both natural and man-made.

With over 150, power-packed, articles to choose from, the busy entrepreneur has at their fingertips, bite-sized training lessons to help them on their success journey. There is so much information packed into this book that it could well be the only book on core business issues that you will ever need.

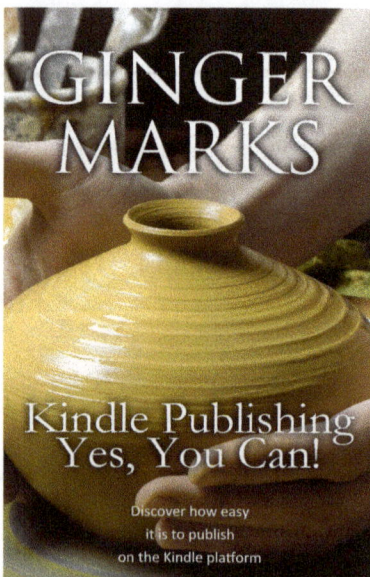

Publishing your ebook doesn't guarantee your book will look the way you intended it to. Even using the auto-generation tools can result in an ebook that isn't laid out the way you created it. In *Kindle Publishing, Yes You Can*, Ginger Marks, publisher and designer, explains in easy terms exactly what you need to do and how to create an ebook that you will be proud to call your own.

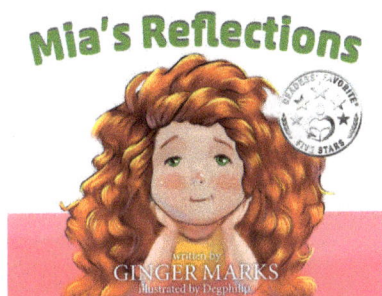

Ginger's first children's picture book, *Mia's Reflections,* captures the heart of a young girl who learns that beauty is not just a pretty face, but rather a giving life.

Anticipating a new school with no friends, where she feels alone and ugly, young Mia prepares for her first day. She steps near her Grandmother's old Cheval mirror and there she senses her mama reaching out to her. "You're not ugly," her mama says. "You're beautiful." And she traces all the beautiful services Mia performs in a day. At last her mother appears in the mirror to give a fresh look at Mia's loveliness.

Followed by Parent/Teacher resources, this book will fill a young girl's day with thoughts of love and kindness.

$6.99 eBook Edition

$14.99 Print Edition (Feb 2019)

Book trailer: https://youtu.be/4DoQe9zp8LY

# Weird and Wacky Holiday Marketing Guide Archive

All previous Editions Available at http://www.HolidayMarketingGuide.com/past.html
including the *Companion Playguide*.